Canto is an imprint offering a range of titles, classic and more recent, across a broad spectrum of subject areas and interests. History, literature, biography, archaeology, politics, religion, psychology, philosophy and science are all represented in Canto's specially selected list of titles, which now offers some of the best and most accessible of Cambridge publishing to a wider readership.

THE BYZANTINE LADY: TEN PORTRAITS

DONALD M. NICOL

THE BYZANTINE LADY
TEN PORTRAITS
1250–1500

CAMBRIDGE
UNIVERSITY PRESS

Published by the Press Syndicate of the University of Cambridge
The Pitt Building, Trumpington Street, Cambridge CB2 1RP
40 West 20th Street, New York, NY 10011–4211, USA
10 Stamford Road, Oakleigh, Melbourne 3166, Australia

First published 1994
Canto edition 1996

Printed in Great Britain at the University Press, Cambridge

A catalogue record for this book is available from the British Library

Library of Congress cataloguing in publication data
Nicol, Donald MacGillivray.
The Byzantine lady: ten portraits, 1250–1500 / Donald M. Nicol.
Includes bibliographical references and index.
ISBN 0 521 45531 6
1. Women – Byzantine Empire – Biography.
2. Upper classes – Byzantine Empire – Biography.
3. Byzantine empresses – Biography.
4. Byzantine Empire – Civilization – 1081–1453.
I. Title.
DF633.3.N53   1994
949.5'04'0922 – dc20   93–35728   CIP
[B]

ISBN 0 521 45531 6 hardback
ISBN 0 521 57623 7 paperback

CONTENTS

PLATES

Between pages 54 and 55

PREFACE

About ninety years ago the distinguished French historian Charles Diehl published two volumes of biographical vignettes of prominent Byzantines, male and female, under the title *Figures Byzantines*. Some of the imperial ladies among them were reprinted in 1959 as *Impératrices de Byzance*. More recently, in 1988, Sir Dimitri Obolensky published his *Six Byzantine Portraits*, all, as it happens, male. These books are my models for this small offering. I cannot compete with the scholarly eloquence of either Diehl or Obolensky. But whereas the former did not sully the charm of his pages with any notes or references to his sources, the latter cites chapter and verse for almost every statement in his text. I feel that this is helpful and have therefore followed his lead. Most of the material for this book was gathered in the Gennadius Library in Athens; and I would like to express my gratitude to the staff of that incomparable institution. It was finished in or near Cambridge. I must particularly thank Pauline Del Mar for her help in generating a legible typescript. Finally, I owe a debt yet again to the care and efficiency of the Cambridge University Press.

ABBREVIATIONS

INTRODUCTION

THE BYZANTINE EMPIRE, radiating out from its capital at Constantinople, the Queen of Cities, lasted for about 1100 years. It was the longest-lived political institution of the middle ages. Its people and their rulers were conservative by instinct. Their conservatism is reflected in their art and their literature. What God had revealed in the incarnation of his son, in the virgin birth and in the resurrection set fixed standards for artists. The patterns for depicting these revelations were immutable, save for minor variations. It would be dangerous to alter them. The standards for literature were set by the style and language of the ancient Greeks transmuted into acceptable Christian form. These models of life and thought and letters would never change. For the Empire and its church were ordained and protected by God and were destined to last for ever, or at least until the second coming of Christ and the end of this vale of tears. None the less, in so long a span of years, there were changes in society, some subtle and barely observed as they occurred, others more disturbing and more noticeable at the time, affecting the security, the economy and the extent of the empire.

Being conservative by nature, many Byzantines felt, as pessimists generally do, that all change was for the worse, especially in the familiar and hallowed customs of their Christian society. A regular euphemism for heresy in the church was 'innovation' or novelty. The same was true for the disquieting manifestations of change in daily life and social customs. A fourteenth-century historian complains about the foreign and bizarre forms of headgear being worn in Constantinople in his day. Such laments are part of the stock in trade of the middle-aged or elderly seeing portents of the world's end in changes of fashion by the younger generation. Changes in thought and in social activity are another matter.

In the last centuries of Byzantium there were many such changes.

One was in the attitude towards women in society and women's own perception of their place therein. I have singled out ten individuals to illustrate the point. It may be objected that they were all proud to belong to the aristocracy. This is inevitable; the source material dictates the choice; one cannot construct biographies of persons who left no records but their names. The ten women whose lives I have here described would have preferred to be called Ladies, for they were all conscious of having been born into an exalted class of society. Their birth or their marriage assured them the right to certain well-defined privileges of title and rank. If it were not so, we would not know so much about them. The available contemporary sources are relatively uninformative about the lives and deeds of humbler women in the cities and villages of the late Byzantine Empire. Their upper-class sisters in Constantinople or Thessalonica are better documented and in any case rather more interesting. The registers of the Patriarchate of Constantinople in the fourteenth century report many case histories of women who took their grievances before the ecclesiastical courts. The lives of saints too provide revealing glimpses of the life of women in Byzantine society. But such piecemeal information seldom provides enough material to compile a biography of the person concerned. Some archival documents too, especially concerning landed estates owned by the great monasteries of Mount Athos and elsewhere, provide incidental evidence for the lives of peasant families which can be extrapolated into statistics. They show, as one would expect, that the wives and daughters of farmers, shepherds and country priests led hard and generally dull lives. It was the city ladies who made the news; and it is the fleeting records of their lives that indicate a change away from the previously accepted stereotype of the secluded, bashful, docile, male-dominated woman in Byzantine society.

The change was noted and disliked by the church. Old-fashioned and fanatical bishops and monks, in the style of St John Chrysostom, or of John Knox, thought that women should be seen and not heard. The Patriarch Athanasios I, about 1300, inveighs against the high-society ladies who went to the cathedral of the Holy Wisdom with painted faces and tricked out in gold and jewellery simply to make an insolent show of themselves. The saintly monk Athanasios of the Meteora went so far as to say that women should not even be seen and ran away when he saw one of them coming. Woman for him was the 'affliction, the powerhouse of passion for those addicted to the flesh'. Another of the fourteenth-century Patriarchs of Constantinople, Philotheos, condemns the crowds of superficial and empty-headed ladies of the aristocracy in his city who combine their vaunted nobility with vacuousness and a fondness for creating schism in the church, thereby acquiring notoriety and a following. This is the not very Christian spite of one who became a saint of the Orthodox church. But there was a revealing and interesting element of truth in his ravings. For in the thirteenth and fourteenth centuries Byzantine women seemed to feel more free and more confident to do and to say things than their ancestors. Byzantine society remained, as it had always been, patriarchal in all senses of the word. It had often, however, produced powerful and domineering ladies, as empresses, princesses, mothers and nuns. Among the most famous examples were Justinian's Empress Theodora; the blue-stocking princess Anna Comnena; and the Empress Eirene at the end of the eighth century, who reigned as Emperor in her own right and very nearly married Charlemagne.

They were exceptional; but that is what empresses and princesses are supposed to be; and it is for this reason that later generations knew so much more about them than they cared to know about the wives and daughters of the peasantry. They were above average in thought, word and deed. The Byzantines were incurable snobs. Their historians, writing for the most part in a highly sophisticated form of Greek far removed from their spoken language, have little to tell about the ordinary men and women of their day. Their history was made by top people. They regarded democracy as a dirty word and a dangerous concept, Greek though it was. For them monarchy was the only sensible form of government. The dramatis personae of their narratives were emperors, courtiers, generals and officials of church and state. Latterly their top people came to include those of substantial means and influence whom they called 'the well-born', 'the powerful', or the golden élite. Heredity came to have a greater significance than merit. In earlier ages of Byzantine society surnames or family names were not of much importance. A great Emperor like Basil I (867–86) trailed no clouds of glory in his ancestry. By the eleventh and twelfth centuries things had changed. Great families of the élite advertised their breeding and their wealth by making sure that their family names were known; and the mothers and wives of those families took to adopting strings of such names to prove their own right to fame. By the fourteenth century the most well-born and influential families were those of Palaiologos and Cantacuzene; and by the fifteenth century almost everyone among the élite was related to one or the other. Thus, the mother of the Emperor John Cantacuzene (1347–54), for all that he was her only child, was proud to style herself Theodora Palaiologina Angelina Cantacuzene.

3

Earlier in the fourteenth century another Theodora Palaiologina, niece of the Emperor Michael VIII, founded a convent of nuns in Constantinople, dedicated to the Virgin of Good Hope. The text of its foundation charter or *typikon* reads like an Almanac de Gotha of the high society of the age. It contains the names and the portraits of Theodora as the nun Theodoule, of her parents, their children and their grandchildren. She is named as Theodora Branaina Komnene Laskarina Cantacuzene Palaiologina, listing all the families with which she was connected by birth or by marriage. All told, eighteen descendants of her father, Constantine Palaiologos, through four generations, are named in this remarkable document. It is a unique advertisement for solidarity among aristocratic families. It illustrates the supreme importance of the family unit in late Byzantine society and of the bonds that held particular families together.

Women, and not only wives and mothers, had come to play a much more public and influential part in the running of society and the Empire. They were expected to behave in a modest and seemly manner. It was still thought improper for ladies to go about on their own and unaccompanied. But they were no longer confined to the women's quarters of their houses and they were not shy of making their opinions known and their voices heard.

The Patriarch Philotheos about 1370 condemned the vacuous noble ladies of Constantinople for taking sides in the religious controversies of the time and creating schism in the church. Such controversies, often about abstruse points of theology, had been a substitute for politics in Byzantium at least from the time of the Empress Theodora in the sixth century. Theodora had favoured the cause of the Monophysite party in the church which her husband Justinian and the Orthodox Christians denounced as heretical. In 787 and again in 842 empresses had changed the course of church history by clearly pronouncing on the disputed subject of the veneration of icons in Christian worship. But as a general rule women, however exalted, were not expected to state their views on such matters. In the thirteenth and fourteenth centuries, however, aristocratic ladies played an extraordinarily active part in opposing official imperial policy in ecclesiastical affairs, even courting persecution for their beliefs. The Emperor Michael VIII Palaiologos, in trying to enforce union with the church of Rome on his mainly unwilling subjects, made implacable enemies of several of his own female relatives. Notable among them were his sister Eirene, the nun Eugenia, and her daughter Theodora Raoulaina (no. 3 below). They were both exiled for their rebellious outspokenness. They showed a strength of spirit and honesty of conscience which put many of their time-serving male contemporaries to shame.

Many of them were also extremely well off in terms of hereditary wealth and landed property. Theodora Cantacuzene was able to finance her son's bid for the throne and to pay his soldiers out of her own purse. They were quite competent to manage their own estates for the benefit of their families; and some, like Theodora's daughter-in-law Eirene (no. 6), showed themselves capable of defending and governing outposts of empire when their husbands were absent. Eirene Cantacuzene was a most dutiful and courageous wife and her husband's most loyal and obedient supporter. She never lost sight of the fact that a married woman's chief concern was the welfare of her family. Women like her in the fourteenth century did not question the accepted morality that the prime purpose of marriage was the procreation of children, and that motherhood was the most privileged function of a woman. Byzantine society might still be patriarchal; but the mother ruled the household and the family and took immense pride in doing so. Byzantine law allowed her considerable freedom in the management of economic affairs in the family. The dowry that came to her on marriage was specifically designed to promote the well-being of her children and it remained almost inalienable from her. A woman could take her husband to court for appropriating it or mismanaging it.

The ideal of a Christian marriage made in heaven and blest with issue was of course not often realised. Love matches between partners of the right families were rare. Betrothals followed by marriages were arranged not in heaven but around the financial or diplomatic table by parents keen to see that their daughters benefited themselves and their families in the most profitable way. The dowry system made arranged marriages convenient if not inevitable; and in these matters it was generally the paterfamilias and not the mother whose will prevailed. Daughters, unlike sons, were considered to be expendable commodities for diplomatic or economic purposes. The canonical age for marriage was twelve for a girl and fourteen (or sixteen) for a boy. At such an age neither partner could object, although as a rule the men were much older than their almost child brides and were sometimes widowers. The most scandalous case of such a union was that of Simonis Palaiologina, the five-year-old daughter of the Emperor Andronikos II, who was obliged to marry the fifty-year-old Kral of Serbia, Stephen Milutin, in 1299. The church objected most vigorously; and the consequences were disastrous for the health and happiness of poor little Simonis. But she was sacrificed for the supposed good of the Empire.

She was not the first nor the last to be so exploited. Even the Ottoman Turks could be mollified and kept at bay by marriage to a well-endowed Byzantine princess. The Emperor John VI gave his daughter Theodora as wife to Orhan, Emir of Bithynia. George Branković, Despot of Serbia in the fifteenth century, married off his daughter Mara to the Ottoman Sultan Murad II (no. 9). The Christian Emperors of Trebizond on the Black Sea kept their little enclave free from attack by giving their daughters in marriage to their pagan or infidel neighbours (no. 10). In an earlier age the Byzantine rulers of northern Greece, the Despots of Epiros, tried to preserve their independence from the Emperors in Constantinople by arranging marriages for their daughters with the Italian princes across the water. Thus it was that Helena Doukaina (no. 1), daughter of the Despot of Epiros, became the wife of Manfred of Hohenstaufen, King of the Two Sicilies, in 1259; and Thamar of Epiros was married to Philip of Anjou, Prince of Taranto, in 1294 (no. 2). Eight of the eleven female members of the ruling families in Greece in the thirteenth century married either Italian or Frankish husbands; though not a single male member took a foreign wife. Daughters were useful pawns in the diplomatic game. Those thus used or misused were seldom happy in their married lives. Very rarely did a daughter summon up the courage to disobey her parents' wishes. One was Mara Branković of Serbia (no. 9), who refused to be considered as a bride for the last Byzantine Emperor, Constantine XI Palaiologos. But she was an older woman and a widow; and she had done her bit by spending sixteen years in the harem of the Sultan Murad.

Two of the Italian ladies who married Emperors of Constantinople became byzantinised to the extent of adopting the Orthodox faith and never returning to their homelands, though both were headstrong and ambitious by nature (nos. 4 and 7). They were ambitious for their children, especially for their sons as heirs apparent to the throne. They loved their sons more than they cared for their husbands. Many a Byzantine Empress had to endure the indignity of her husband's infidelity. The number of illegitimate children fathered by the pious Christian Emperors of the Romans is surprising. Michael VIII, Andronikos II and Andronikos III each admitted to two daughters born out of wedlock. Manuel II, who wrote a Dialogue on Christian marriage, admitted the same. Illegitimate daughters too had their uses for diplomatic purposes, for they could be married off with tempting dowries to lesser and potentially troublesome foreigners on the frontiers of the Empire. Michael VIII successfully disposed of his bastard daughters by marrying one to Nogaj, Khan of the Golden Horde of the Mongols in south Russia, the other to a son of Hulagu, Khan of the Mongols in Persia. Andronikos II followed his example. The Mongols were no doubt flattered to be included in the imperial family of Constantinople even at one remove. The Emperor John V made the mistake of begetting an illegitimate son, who was not so easy to dispose of and who ended his days after seventeen years in prison. The Emperor Andronikos III, who married Anna of Savoy (no. 7), gave one of his illegitimate girls as wife to the Emperor of Trebizond, Basil I, the other to Uzbeq, Khan of the Golden Horde. It is interesting to note how useful the Mongols were as recipients of the Emperors' unwanted progeny.

The last resort for a slighted wife was divorce. Divorce had always been permissible in Byzantine law on certain clearly specified and well-defined grounds based on Roman law as adapted to Christian usage by Justinian and his successors. The interpretation of the law in numerous cases kept the lawyers, the canonists and the ecclesiastical tribunals busy during the later centuries of Byzantine society. But for the most part innocent wives were well protected socially and financially from husbands who had wronged them. The legal emphasis was always on the welfare of the children and their mother. Divorce was a rare event, however, among the ladies of the aristocracy, and on the whole they were noted for their devotion and loyalty to their husbands. There were two other options open to women of means who could no longer stand their husbands: one was to live apart from them; the other was to enter a convent. The Empress Eirene of Montferrat and after her the Empress Anna of Savoy (nos. 4 and 7) preferred to live in the city of Thessalonica at a distance from their husbands in Constantinople. The princess Eirene Choumnaina (no. 5), having become a childless widow early in life, preferred not to marry again and became a nun in the convent which she founded in Constantinople.

If to become a successful wife and mother of a family was woman's most glorious fulfilment on this earth, to become a bride of Christ promised spiritual fulfilment in this world and the next. A fully professed and tonsured monk or nun put on what the Byzantines called 'the angelic habit' of the monastic estate, the highest calling available to human kind. Several convents of nuns were founded or restored in Constantinople in the thirteenth and fourteenth centuries. Elderly or widowed ladies would often retire to such institutions as nuns, there to die in the angelic habit. Some of them were rich and their financial contributions to the repair and upkeep of their convents were welcome. Nor were their vows of poverty and obedience too severely pressed upon them. They led elegant and sheltered lives which reminded them more of their aristocratic or imperial past in the world than of monastic impoverishment. For, as one abbess remarked, virtue comes more easily in well-appointed surroundings. Life in the convent was something like an extension of the family. There were indeed some who thought that the over-privileged nuns, who seldom soiled their hands with corporal works of mercy, were rather too worldly and too attached to the families of their own whom they were supposed to have put behind them. One such was the foundress of the convent of Good Hope with her obsessive attachment to her lineage and family connexions. Another was Eirene Choumnaina (no. 5), who could never forget that she had briefly been married to the heir to the throne.

Many of these ladies of the veil were highly intelligent and well educated by the standards of female literacy in Byzantium. In the western world in the middle ages literacy was generally a prerogative of the monks and clergy who, as a class, maintained the continuity of education and scholarship albeit, as in Byzantium, through the medium of a dead language. To be able to sign one's name was a mark of literacy, a talent which, as Anna Comnena observed, was denied to all the leaders of the First Crusade except for the bishops. The rate of literacy among the laity, though by no means universal, was always higher in the Byzantine world. But women were not expected and not trained to be literate to any sophisticated degree. Anna Comnena herself was a striking exception. The thirteenth and fourteenth centuries in Byzantium witnessed a remarkable revival of Greek scholarship, a resurgence of literary and philosophical interest in the classical Greek heritage of the past. It has been called 'the last Byzantine Renaissance'. Its leading lights, one of whom was Nikephoros Choumnos, the erudite father of the nun Eirene-Eulogia, were men, educated by men, as one would suppose. The evidence for the education of women in this age is minimal, though it is clear that the daughters of the aristocracy at least were taught more than the rudiments of literacy, probably by private tuition; and no doubt the scholarly activities and interests of so many of their fathers affected them and inspired them to make their own forays into scholarship. Eirene-Eulogia was one of them; but the outstanding blue-stocking princess of the time was Theodora Raoulaina (no. 3) who, though a nun, sought and merited the friendship of several of the leading scholars of the Byzantine renaissance. She collected a library of her own, copied manuscripts with her own hand, wrote lives of saints, and ran a workshop of scribes and artists in her convent.

In the latter part of the fourteenth century the renaissance began to lose its force. The promising rediscovery of the treasures of ancient

Greek learning and literature degenerated into pedantry. The church had in any case disapproved of it. In a world that seemed to be collapsing, religious certainty took precedence over the dangerous speculations of pagan writers of antiquity. Byzantine society withdrew into its earlier reclusiveness and nervous isolationism. About 1450 Aeneas Sylvius, the future Pope Pius II, declared that no Latin or westerner could consider himself to be properly educated unless he had studied for a time in Constantinople. He was living in the past. The true state of affairs was revealed by Gennadios Scholarios, the future Patriarch of Constantinople, who sadly declared that only three or four people in the city were any longer concerned with learning, and that of a very superficial nature.

The stagnation of Byzantine culture, literature and the arts seems to be reflected in a reversion of the role and status of women in society. The ladies of the court and high society, who had for a time enjoyed a little more respect for their opinions and their abilities outside the closed circle of the household or the convent, grimly watched the lights going out as the Turks moved in on Constantinople. Their wealth was disappearing. They could no longer afford to deck themselves out in finery to go to church. They could no longer afford to found elegant convents for their retirement. By 1400 Asia Minor, where landed estates had filled the coffers of aristocratic families, was already Turkey. The vast properties once owned by the Cantacuzene family in Thrace and Macedonia were overrun by the Turks. The only stable element left in the lives of the once proud Byzantine ladies was the family unit and the bonds of marriage and kinship that held families together. These they struggled to preserve as a means of survival. Marriageable daughters still had their uses. A daughter with her dowry might melt the heart even of a conquering Sultan.

Francesco Filelfo, the Italian humanist, who lived and studied in Constantinople in the 1420s and married a Byzantine lady, noted with sadness, and perhaps with truth, that the aristocratic ladies of the city lived secluded lives, meeting no one except close relatives and never venturing out of doors except after dark and with their faces veiled. After the Turkish conquest in 1453 it was all dark. Some of the dynamism and independence of spirit of earlier Byzantine ladies, however, lived on in some of their descendants. Anna Notaras (no. 8) spent most of her long life in Venice and devoted herself to the cause of the Greek refugees from Constantinople after the conquest. Mara Branković (no. 9) lived out her life in what had become Turkey as the much-respected Christian stepmother of the conquering Sultan Mehmed II. She did not

9

melt his heart but she had a benign and civilising influence on him. Poor Helena Cantacuzene (no. 10), however, was his victim. Like the tragic princess Helena Doukaina (no. 1), she had no influence on anyone, except perhaps on the souls of her family.

The ten ladies whose biographies I have here sketched all lived between the years 1250 and 1500. The sources which I have used, both contemporary and modern, are listed in the footnotes and the bibliography for those who might like to know more. They may serve to illustrate some of the advantages and disadvantages of dynastic and diplomatic marriages in the late Byzantine world; some of the joys, trials and tribulations of being a nun or a scholar; some of the delights and pitfalls of being an ambitious mother or an embittered wife; some of the problems and unexpected benefits of being the wife and widow of a Turkish Sultan, or an unmarried refugee in Italy in the fifteenth century. I have tried to set each lady in her historical context so that readers may understand something of the social, political and religious influences that shaped her life. Above all, I have tried to dispel some of the gloom about the role of Byzantine women in their own Christian, medieval society, so endurable and familiar to them, so alien and intolerable to us.

CHAPTER ONE

———— ✜ ————

HELENA DOUKAINA,
QUEEN OF THE TWO SICILIES,
1258–1266

IN the golden age of the Byzantine Empire it was thought improper
that a true 'Roman' or Byzantine should marry a foreigner. Constantine Porphyrogenitus in the tenth century had strongly advised his
son against arranging marriage alliances between members of the
imperial family and spouses of any other nation. He made exception
only for the 'Franks', on the spurious ground that Constantine the Great
had come from the Frankish world.[1] Two hundred years later the
Emperors could no longer afford to be so ethnically pure. The fiction
that the true Romans of Byzantium were a race apart from the rest of
the Christian world was untenable. Four of the five Emperors of the
dynasty of Komenos in the twelfth century married western Christian
or Latin wives.[2] The blood that flowed in the veins of the last imperial
dynasty, the Palaiologi, was far from purely 'Roman'. The last Christian Roman Emperor of Constantinople, Constantine Palaiologos, who
died defending the walls of his city against the Turks in 1453, was
Serbian on his mother's side and half-Italian on his father's side, with a
dash of Hungarian and Armenian blood contributed by his ancestors.[3]
In the last centuries of Byzantium diplomatic marriages and the dowries
that went with them became a means of survival among the ruling
classes.

After the catastrophe of the Fourth Crusade in 1204 and the estab-
lishment of the so-called Latin Empire of Constantinople by the Franks
and Venetians, the rulers of the Byzantine Empire in exile at Nicaea
were naturally averse to making marital alliances with their foreign

[1] Constantine Porphyrogenitus, *De Administrando Imperio*, ed. and trans. R. J. H. Jenkins
and Gy. Moravcsik, 2nd ed. (Washington, D.C., 1967), chap. 13, pp. 70–6.
[2] C. Diehl, 'Princesses d'Occident à la cour des Comnènes', in Diehl, *Figures byzantines*,
ser. II (Paris, 1908), pp. 164–206.
[3] D. M. Nicol, *The Immortal Emperor. The life and legend of Constantine Palaiologos, last
emperor of the Romans* (Cambridge, 1992).

conquerors. They strove to maintain their exclusivity in the imperial family of Laskaris. The Emperor John III Vatatzes, however, looking for a willing ally against the Latins in Constantinople, married Constance, the young daughter of Frederick II of Hohenstaufen.[4] The victims of such marital alliances were almost always the female partners and their offspring who were exploited as pawns in the game of diplomacy. They and their lords and masters accepted this as a fact of life. Only rarely were the consequences tragic.

The rival Byzantine claimants to the liberation and possession of Constantinople were the rulers of Epiros in north-western Greece who, like the Emperors in exile at Nicaea, had resisted the Latin invaders of the Empire since 1204. Their territory came to be known as the Despotate of Epiros, centred around the cities of Arta in the south and Ioannina in the north. It was a tragedy for the Byzantine world that its two states in exile could never co-operate or combine their forces to expel the foreign intruders from the capital of the Empire which each aspired to possess. In the end their jealous rivalry had to be fought out in open warfare in 1259. The victory went to the Emperors of Nicaea and two years later they complemented it by recovering the city of Constantinople. The new Emperor of the Romans was Michael VIII Palaiologos, who moved his capital from Nicaea to Constantinople in August 1261.[5]

The coastline of Epiros and Albania had often suffered from its geographical position. It was the part of the Byzantine Empire nearest to the south of Italy. In the eleventh and twelfth centuries the Normans from Apulia and Sicily knew that the sea route eastwards opened the gateway to the road over the mountains of Epiros and Macedonia to Thessalonica and Constantinople. In the middle of the thirteenth century the way that the Normans had shown was to be followed by a new contender. The Despot of Epiros at the time was Michael Komnenos Doukas, the second of that name to rule his principality from his capital at Arta. Like the Emperor at Nicaea, Michael had tried with some success to cultivate the friendship of the German Emperor Frederick II of Hohenstaufen, who counted Sicily and southern Italy among his provinces. When Frederick died in 1250 he left the Kingdom of the Two Sicilies to his elder son Conrad and the Principality of Taranto to his other son Manfred. On Conrad's death in 1254 the succession passed

[4] G. Schlumberger, 'Le tombeau d'une impératrice Byzantine à Valence en Espagne', *Byzance et Croisades. Pages médiévales* (Paris, 1927), pp. 56–86; C. Diehl, 'Constance de Hohenstaufen Impératrice de Nicée', in Diehl, *Figures byzantines* ser. II, pp. 207–25.

[5] D. J. Geanakoplos, *Emperor Michael Palaeologus and the West 1258–1282* (Cambridge, Mass., 1959).

to his infant son Conradin and Manfred assumed the regency until such time as he could appropriate the crown. His coronation as King of Sicily took place at Palermo in August 1258. Frederick II had felt sympathetic towards the Greeks. His son Manfred of Sicily inherited the ambitions of his Norman predecessors in the direction of Byzantium. Towards the end of 1257 he took his first step towards realising those ambitions by sending a fleet over the Adriatic to attack and acquire part of the coastline of northern Epiros and Albania. In June 1258 he sent reinforcements across the water; and before long he had made himself suzerain of all the coast from Durazzo south to Kanina as well as the island of Corfu. He appointed his admiral, a Cypriote Frank called Philip Chinardo, as governor of his overseas possessions.[6]

The Despot of Epiros, Michael II, had been taken unawares. He was in Macedonia busily preparing for his fight to the death with the army of his rival the Emperor of Nicaea. He could not make war against different enemies on two sides at once. His priority must be victory over his rival in the east, for that would give him the chance to march on Thessalonica and win back Constantinople from the Latins. It occurred to him that he might resolve his dilemma by soliciting the support of Manfred of Sicily and turning a dangerous enemy into a favoured ally. An alliance could be arranged to the advantage of both parties. The agent of the alliance between the Kingdom of Sicily and the Despotate of Epiros was to be Michael's daughter Helena. The Despot would offer her in marriage to Manfred. In 1258 Helena was about sixteen years old and Manfred about twenty-six. His first wife, Beatrice of Savoy, had died in January of that year. She left him an only daughter, Constance. He would be glad to marry again, especially since it was proposed that the young Helena's dowry would consist of a number of places on the coast of Epiros, thus legitimising his claim to the overseas possessions which he had already taken by conquest. Manfred had nothing to lose by entering into such an agreeable alliance. There was the added incentive that Helena Doukaina was reported to be of rare beauty, charm and wit. They would make a good match. Manfred of Sicily, whatever the Pope may have thought of him, was an attractive and sympathetic character. He inherited many of his father's talents in literature, learning, music and the arts. Dante accused him of manifold sins with regard to the church and true religion yet found a place for him in Purgatory and not in Hell. The Popes were less charitable. For them the family of Hohenstaufen was a brood of vipers.

[6] D. M. Nicol, *The Despotate of Epiros*, I: *1204–1267* (Oxford, 1957), pp. 166–71.

No son of Frederick II, the 'excommunicatissimus', could find their favour.[7]

Manfred had personal reasons for co-operating in what might prove to be the downfall of the Empire of Nicaea. His half-sister Constance of Hohenstaufen had been given as a child bride to the Emperor John III in 1244. He had rejected her in favour of one of her ladies-in-waiting. She was still held as a prisoner at Nicaea and found herself forced to fend off the lecherous advances of the new Emperor Michael VIII.[8] Manfred was no friend of the Emperors of Nicaea. The Roman church would of course object to his taking an Orthodox Christian princess to wife. One of the reasons given for the Pope's excommunication of his father Frederick II in 1245 had been that he gave his daughter Constance in marriage to a ruler who was in schism from the one true church.[9] But the Popes disapproved of almost everything that Frederick and Manfred did and said. Manfred's own motives for making an alliance with the Despot of Epiros were undoubtedly devious. It would save him the trouble of having to defend the territories and islands in northern Greece which he had appropriated; and he might after all find himself on the winning side when it came to the reconquest of Constantinople. The prospect of adding the name of Emperor of the Romans to his other titles was probably somewhere in the back of his mind.[10]

The young Helena Doukaina of Epiros was thus destined to become the Queen of the Two Sicilies. Her betrothal to Manfred was duly announced in 1258 and although her wedding was delayed until the following year her father tactfully refrained from arguing about the terms of her dowry. The details of the contract in its original form have been much disputed. It was frequently cited in later years as political circumstances changed; but it is clear that it was a document of considerable and lasting significance for the future of relations between Italy and Greece, for it signed away to the Kingdom of Sicily a large

---

[7] Nicol, *Despotate of Epiros*, I, p. 171; S. Runciman, *The Sicilian Vespers* (Cambridge, 1958), pp. 26–38; Geanakoplos, *Emperor Michael*, pp. 48, 60. Dante, *Purgatorio*, Canto III. 103–45.

[8] Schlumberger, 'Le tombeau', 73–4; Geanakoplos, *Emperor Michael*, pp. 144–6.

[9] D. M. Nicol, 'Mixed marriages in Byzantium in the thirteenth century', *Studies in Church History*, I, ed. C. W. Dugmore and C. Duggan (London and Edinburgh, 1964), pp. 164–5 (reprinted in Nicol, *Byzantium: its ecclesiastical history and relations with the western world* (London, 1972), no. IV).

[10] B. Berg, 'Manfred of Sicily and the Greek East', *Byzantina*, XIV (1988), 263–89, is inclined to play down Manfred's imperialistic designs on Constantinople. See E. Merendino, 'Manfredi tra Epiro e Nicea', *Actes du XVe Congrès International d'Etudes byzantines*, IV (Athens, 1980), pp. 245–52.

part of what had for centuries been Byzantine territory in Epiros and Albania.[11]

There was a third party to the grand alliance of the Despot Michael II against Nicaea. William of Villehardouin, the French Prince of Achaia in the Peloponnese, was an experienced and adventurous soldier who enjoyed fighting. In June 1258 he restored order among his own rebellious barons. He was at the height of his career and ready for further bellicose adventures. Michael of Epiros suggested that he should join forces with the Despotate in the war against Nicaea. The alliance would be strengthened by another marriage. Michael's younger daughter Anna was now of marriageable age and no less attractive than her sister Helena. William of Villehardouin had been a widower for nearly three years. The prospect of taking a third wife and perhaps of extending his Principality into northern Greece as a consequence appealed to him. Ambassadors were exchanged. The dowry was agreed. Anna would bring to her husband 60,000 gold coins, a castle and lands in southern Thessaly, and sumptuous gifts. The wedding took place without delay at Patras in the summer of 1258, Anna being given away by her brother Nikephoros. Oaths of mutual assistance between the Despot of Epiros and the Prince of Achaia rendered them 'as one man'; and the beautiful Anna, 'like a second Helen with her Menelaus', was escorted to Villehardouin's new castle at Mistra in the Peloponnese.[12]

It would be interesting to know how the mother of Helena and Anna felt about the marriage of her daughters. She had a reputation for virtue and sanctity and is to this day revered as a saint in the city of Arta where she died as a nun. Her name was Theodora and she came of the originally Norman family of Petraliphas. In earlier days she had had ample occasion to learn the virtues of tolerance and forgiveness, for her husband Michael had treated her badly. He had banished her to exile when he became ensnared by the wiles of an adulteress. After five years he realised that he had been bewitched and corrupted and restored the saintly Theodora to favour. To atone for his sins he endowed at least two churches in Arta. Theodora's biography leaves no doubt about her sanctity and forbearance. But it records almost nothing about her part

---

[11] On the extent of her dowry, see D. M. Nicol, *The Despotate of Epiros*, II: *1267–1479* (Cambridge, 1984), p. 13. There are two substantial studies on Helena and her marriage to Manfred: G. Del Giudice, 'La famiglia di Re Manfredi', *ASPN*, III (1878), 3–80; IV (1879), 35–110, 290–352; V (1880), 21–95, 262–323, 470–547 (Also printed separately (Naples, 1896)). M. A. Dendias, Ἑλένη Ἀγγελίνα Δούκαινα Βασίλισσα Σικελίας καὶ Νεαπόλεως, Ἠπειρωτικὰ Χρονικά, I (1926), 219–94. See also Geanakoplos, *Emperor Michael*, pp. 47–54.

[12] Nicol, *Despotate of Epiros*, I, pp. 172–3.

in the political schemes of her devious if repentant husband. She bore him three sons and three daughters. But she had little say in their destinies after their childhood. She must have been pleased that her daughter Anna, as wife of the prince of Achaia, was at least still on Greek soil. Poor little Helena on the other hand was to be whisked off to Italy where she would be a stranger in a strange land. Had her mother known what Helena's future as Queen of Sicily would be she would have been even more distressed.[13]

Arrangements for Helena's wedding to Manfred were concluded in the spring of 1259. In May a fleet of ships arrived from Italy to take her to the port of Trani on the coast of Apulia where Manfred was awaiting her. She sailed accompanied by a retinue of knights and ladies both Italian and Greek. The Byzantine sources do no more than report the event of the marriage. There is, however, one anonymous account written in the Apulian dialect by a citizen of Trani who was there at the time.[14] For him it was a great, joyous and memorable occasion. 'On 2 June of the same year [1259]', he writes,

> there arrived in Apulia eight galleys bringing the betrothed of the lord and King Manfred, the daughter of the Despot of Epiros, by name Helena, accompanied by many barons and lords from our kingdom as well as from the land of her father. She disembarked at the harbour at Trani where the king was waiting for her. As soon as the girl alighted from her ship the king took her in his arms and warmly embraced her. After he had taken her all around our city to the welcoming applause of all the people, they led her to the castle where great feastings and receptions took place. In the evening there were so many lantern bearers and torches lighting up all the streets that it seemed like daylight. On the next day the king ennobled many knights, among them our fellow citizens Cola Pelaganne and Fredericu Sifula, who had been with the queen (*basilissa*) on her voyage in the two ships from our city.

As to Helena's personal charms the chronicler observes that she was most presentable, well mannered and more beautiful than Manfred's first wife. She was said to be no more than seventeen years of age. The crowds that gathered to gaze wherever she went were enchanted by her grace and beauty and loved her dearly. It must be assumed that she was crowned as Queen of Sicily after her wedding in the cathedral of Trani,

---

[13] The biography or hagiography of Helena's mother Theodora was written by the thirteenth-century monk Job (Melias Iasites). See *PLP*, IV, no. 7959.

[14] Extracts from the Anonymus Tranensis (Anonymous of Trani), now apparently lost, were published by D. Forges-Davanzati, in his *Dissertazione sulla seconda moglie del Re Manfredi e su' loro figlioli* (Naples, 1791). Its authenticity has been defended most recently by B. Berg, 'Manfred of Sicily', 248–9.

for her husband had been proclaimed and crowned as King in August 1258. Through her marriage she also acquired the titles of Duchess of Apulia and Princess of Taranto. Her first residence was the imposing castle at Trani which had been built by Manfred's father Frederick II.

The anonymous chronicler of Trani reports that there was further occasion for rejoicing and illuminations in his city in May 1262 when it was announced that Helena had been delivered of a son. Manfred gave him the name of Enrico after his own grandfather. He was Helena's first child.[15] Manfred's previous wife had borne him a daughter, Constance, who in the same year 1262 married the future Peter III of Aragon, later to become King of Sicily. Helena was also to produce a daughter called Beatrice; and there were two more sons. Their names are variously given by the Italian chroniclers, some of whom assert that they were Manfred's illegitimate offspring, though this may have been because the Pope regarded Manfred's marriage to Helena as wholly uncanonical. The second son was named Frederick after his grandfather. The name of the third son is recorded as Azzolino, Aczolinus or Enzio, which has been interpreted as Anselmus. It has been suggested that this should be read as Angelinus or Angelus, implying that Helena's youngest son bore the name of her own family and forebears in Epiros.[16] The fate of Helena's sons was to be so obscure and dismal that their names hardly matter.

From the date of her marriage in June 1259 Helena was to be the consort of Manfred of Sicily for seven years. Not long after her wedding the coalition that her father Michael of Epiros had planned against his rival from Nicaea was put to the test in a confrontation at Pelagonia in Macedonia. It was hardly a battle. William of Villehardouin brought his feudal army north from Achaia and joined forces with his father-in-law Michael in Epiros. Michael's other son-in-law Manfred did not appear in person but he honoured his alliance with Helena's father by sending over a contingent of four hundred German cavalry. The army of Nicaea, fighting to defend Thessalonica and the approaches to Constantinople, had the advantage of being under the unified command of John Palaiologos, brother of the new Emperor Michael VIII. The coalition that Helena's father had stitched together had no centralised control and fell to pieces even before battle was joined. Its leaders quarrelled among themselves. The Despot Michael's bastard son John Doukas fell out with Villehardouin and deserted.

---

[15] Anon. Tranensis, pp. 11–13. Dendias, 248–9.
[16] Dendias, 254–6. On the disputed legitimacy of Manfred's sons, see H. Wieruszowski, 'La Corte di Pietro d'Aragona', *ASI*, anno 96, vol. 1 (1938), 142–3 and notes.

Michael himself with his eldest son Nikephoros decamped in the night leaving their allies to fend for themselves. What battle there was at Pelagonia was left to the French and German troops supplied by Villehardouin and Manfred. They fought with the desperation of men betrayed and they were defeated. Manfred's men were rounded up and surrendered. Villehardouin was found hiding near Kastoria and taken prisoner. John Palaiologos followed up his victory by marching south, while his colleague Alexios Strategopoulos invaded Epiros and captured Arta. The Despot Michael and his son Nikephoros took refuge on the offshore island of Cephalonia.[17]

The victory of the army of Nicaea at Pelagonia in 1259 cleared the air for the reconquest of Constantinople from the Latins. The long expected event occurred two years later, in July 1261, when Alexios Strategopoulos, who had occupied Arta after the battle, led his troops into the city. Otherwise little had changed. Before the end of the year the Despot Michael, Helena's father, had crossed over from his island refuge and fought his way back into the capital of his Despotate at Arta together with his son Nikephoros. His other son John Doukas had repented of his desertion of his father's cause at Pelagonia and returned to Epiros to seek forgiveness. In December Michael sent Nikephoros over to Italy to report to his ally Manfred and to ask for reinforcements. Manfred was no doubt distressed at the loss of his four hundred German cavalry. But he was concerned to hear that troops from Nicaea had threatened his own interests in northern Epiros by invading the lands that had come to him as part of Helena's dowry. Nikephoros must have been pleased to see his sister who was probably then living at the huge castle of Lucera in Apulia; and perhaps through her he was able to influence her husband. He returned to Arta early in 1260 taking with him a company of Italian soldiers. Michael's other son-in-law, who was not released from captivity until 1262, was not so forgiving for his treatment at Pelagonia. But Manfred's continuing support made it possible for the Despotate of Epiros to preserve its independence from the restored Byzantine Empire and to cry defiance at Michael VIII who was crowned as Emperor in Constantinople in 1261.[18]

Manfred's days were, however, numbered. The collapse of the Latin Empire and the restoration of Byzantine rule in Constantinople had been a grievous blow to many in the west, especially the papacy. The Popes, against all the evidence, had seen the Latin occupation as God's instrument for the union of Christendom under the authority of Rome.

---

[17] On the battle of Pelagonia, see Geanakoplos, *Emperor Michael*, pp. 47–74.
[18] Nicol, *Despotate of Epiros*, I, pp. 188–9, 195.

The cause of reimposing Roman authority and Latin rule on Constantinople was at once espoused by those whose interests had suffered most, the Venetians, the last Latin Emperor Baldwin II and other westerners who had lost prestige, land and wealth. The Popes Urban IV and Clement IV believed that the cause merited the preaching of a crusade. When turned out of his 'Empire' in 1261 the unhappy and impoverished Baldwin II had fled to Italy, first to the court of his friend Manfred of Sicily and then to Rome. Manfred was sympathetic and the Pope, Urban IV, began to plan a crusade to put Baldwin back on his throne in Constantinople. But no Pope could countenance an offer of help in this sacred mission from the Hohenstaufen Manfred, who seemed impervious to all the anathemas hurled against him. Manfred must first be eliminated and replaced. No amount of special pleading by Baldwin and by Manfred himself would change the Pope's mind. Urban IV addressed himself to the most pious Louis IX of France; and by July 1263 Louis's brother, Charles of Anjou, had been nominated as the papal champion against Manfred and his 'brood of vipers'. In February 1266 Charles defeated and killed Manfred in battle at Benevento and thus became King of Naples and Sicily. With his new kingdom went the towns, islands and territories across the Adriatic in Epiros which had come to Manfred first through conquest and then by his marriage to Helena. It is reported that there were Greek soldiers fighting on Manfred's side at Benevento. If so they must have been sent by Helena's father, the Despot Michael. They were all captured. Charles of Anjou completed his triumph over the Hohenstaufen by defeating the young Conradin, son of the late Conrad and last legitimate heir, in battle at Tagliacozzo in August 1268. French or Angevin control of the Kingdom of Naples and Sicily was now assured. Pope Clement IV, himself a Frenchman, died in November of the same year. The only relicts of Manfred of Hohenstaufen were his young Greek wife Helena and the four babies in her care.[19]

The contemporary Italian sources and records give differing accounts and scattered allusions to the fate of the widowed Helena after the death of her husband. They are agreed, however, that it was tragic. When the news of the battle at Benevento reached her at the end of February 1266 she seems to have been at Lucera in Apulia living with her daughter and three sons under the protection of the city's garrison commander. Her daughter Beatrice was about five years old, her sons Enrico, Frederick and Azzolino even younger. Also with her was Constance, Manfred's

[19] Runciman, The Sicilian Vespers, pp. 91–5, 109–10.

sister and widow of John III of Nicaea who had finally been released from her long captivity in the east and from the attentions of the Emperor Michael VIII.[20] Helena was put under arrest by the soldiers of Charles of Anjou. She had no idea what to do. Her first instinct was to try to get home to Greece. But no one would come to her support. The barons and courtiers in Lucera turned their backs on her. She was alone and desperate, pining for the husband she had truly loved and sick with worry for the safety of her now fatherless children. The anonymous chronicler of Trani records that only two good men came forward to comfort her, Amerusio and Manualdo with his wife Amundilla. They advised her to make her escape to Trani where they could find her a ship to take her and her children over to her parents in Epiros. The good Amerusio at once got in touch with his friend Lupone in Trani secretly to prepare a galley or some smaller boat and to have it ready. On the night of 3 March her friends escorted Helena and her children down to Trani. Her sister-in-law Constance had suffered enough in the Byzantine world and had no desire to be taken to Greece. She preferred to stay in Italy and face whatever the future might bring her as a prisoner of the Angevins.[21]

Fate was against poor Helena and her children. They arrived at Trani in a violent storm. The sea was rough. There was no hope of setting sail. The keeper of the castle secretly let them in for shelter; and there they had to stay until the weather improved. The secret was not well kept. The chronicler of Trani has it that some monks commissioned by Pope Clement IV as spies to find the late Manfred's friends and relatives discovered the identity of the refugees in the castle and bullied or bribed the keeper into betraying them. He drew up the drawbridge and trapped Helena and her family. On 6 March they with all their jewels and treasures which they had been about to ship to Epiros were handed over to the agents of Charles of Anjou and carried away by night.[22] The chronicler has muddled his facts and his dates. For it is known that Helena was held in the castle at Trani for several months before being taken to Charles's court at Lago Pesole in Basilicata. She may have had happier memories of the place, for it had been a summer residence of Manfred. From there she moved, in the summer of 1266, to the castle of Nocera in Campania. She had stayed there too in happier times. But now she was alone, deprived of the love and company of her children.

[20] Dendias, 264–6.
[21] Anon. Tranensis, pp. 22–3. Del Giudice, 'La famiglia', *ASPN*, IV, 44–58. Constance eventually died in Spain. Schlumberger, 'Le tombeau'.
[22] Dendias, 267–71.

They were removed to a secret destination. Helena was left to linger in solitary confinement.[23] For a time there was talk of finding her a second husband in the person of Henry of Castile, younger brother of King Alfonso X. Charles of Anjou had borrowed money from him for his Italian campaigns and hoped to fob him off with the promise of a young wife and perhaps some land in Epiros. The proposal was soon forgotten. Needless to say, it had not been made for the benefit of the wretched Helena. Its purpose was to suit the political plans of Charles of Anjou, of Pope Clement IV and of her scheming father Michael of Epiros.[24]

The castle on the rock of Nocera de'Cristiani was one of the best fortified and most secure in the realm of Charles of Anjou. Helena had no chance of escaping from it. Its castellan, specially appointed to guard her in 1267, was a French soldier, Rudolfo Fayella or de la Faye. His successor was Enrico de Porta.[25] Charles seemed to be haunted by the ghost of Manfred and obsessed by the fear that his widow might escape. Her three sons, though still mere children, were even more potentially dangerous. They were incarcerated elsewhere. Helena was allowed no freedom but she was not badly treated. She was permitted to have some of her own furniture, carpets, silver candelabras, clothes and jewellery and could at least pretend that she was holding court in some style. She was also allowed to have servants and maids. Records survive of the sums of money that Charles from time to time made over to the castellan of Nocera for the sustenance and upkeep of the former 'Princess of Taranto' in 1269 and 1270.[26] After the death of Conradin at Tagliacozzo in 1268 and the last of her husband's family, she abandoned hope of ever again seeing her freedom or her native land. Henry of Castile, whom she might have been obliged to marry, was taken prisoner at Tagliacozzo and never seen again. Her imprisonment was not much prolonged. She died in February or March 1271, aged barely thirty. Her custodian Enrico de Porta, castellan of Nocera, drew up an inventory of her effects. It was dated 18 July 1271. Her servants and maids were

[23] Del Giudice, 'La famiglia', ASPN, IV, 57–73; V 50–2.

[24] E. G. Léonard, Les Angevins de Naples (Paris, 1954), pp. 64–5; Runciman, Sicilian Vespers, p. 99. Del Giudice, 'La famiglia', ASPN, IV, 82–92, is inclined to doubt that the 'daughter of Michael' offered as bride to Henry of Castile was in fact Helena. Clement V, Les registres de Clément V, ed. E. Jordan, I (Paris, 1893), p. 398, nos. 1164–5. Dendias, 271–82; Geanakoplos, Emperor Michael, pp. 192–3.

[25] Del Giudice, 'La famiglia', ASPN, IV, 299–311; R. Filangieri, I Registri della Cancelleria Angioina, I (Naples, 1950), p. 76.

[26] Filangieri, Registri, I, pp. 280, 283; II, p. 293; III, pp. 36, 74; IV, pp. 25, 217; V, p. 122; VII, pp. 69–70.

dismissed to proceed to their separate destinations under safe conduct. Her goods were sold and the profits paid into the Angevin treasury.[27]

Her daughter Beatrice was no less closely guarded. Some say that she was allowed to stay as a prisoner with her mother at Nocera so long as she was alive. After 1271 she was transferred to Naples where she was confined in the gloomy fortress known as the Castle of the Egg or Castel dell'Uovo, facing the port. She was not harshly treated and, like her mother, enjoyed some limited comforts. There she stayed for some thirteen years until 1284, when, after the collapse of Charles's ambitions in the Sicilian Vespers, she was liberated by the admiral of the Aragonese fleet, Roger de Lauria, and taken to Sicily. There she married Manfred IX, son of the Marquis of Saluzzo.[28]

Helena's three sons, Enrico, Frederick and Azzolino, were condemned to the harshest and most inhuman treatment of all. They were imprisoned in Frederick II's beautiful white tower of Castel del Monte on a lonely height in the district of Bari. They lived in an oblivion of place and time deliberately imposed by Charles of Anjou. They hardly knew their mother and probably never heard of her death in 1271. But in 1272 Enrico and Frederick at least were listed as among the prisoners in the fortress of Castel del Monte. As late as 1298 they were still there and still bound in chains and shackled, surviving on a bare subsistence diet grudgingly doled out to them by their gaoler. Charles of Anjou had hoped that they would die of neglect and starvation. His successors after 1282 seem to have supposed that they were already dead. However, after more than thirty years of oblivion, in 1300 all three were moved to the Castel dell'Uovo in Naples where their sister had been so long confined. The order for their move came from Charles II of Anjou. The long journey on horseback through a countryside that they had never seen proved too much for their stiff and emaciated bodies. Within a year Frederick and Azzolino seem to have died. Only Enrico was left, aged about thirty-eight. He lived as a lonely prisoner for another eighteen years. Nobody knew what to do with him. But nobody would put him out of his misery, still less set him free. He died a miserable death, half-starved, half-witted and probably blind in October 1318 at the age of fifty-six in the dungeons of the Castel dell' Uovo where he had been born. The rumours that he escaped and went

[27] Filangieri, *Registri*, v, p. 271; vi, pp. 203, 378–9. Dendias, 284–5. Del Giudice, 'La famiglia', *ASPN*, iv, 332, says that she died at the end of February or beginning of March 1271. Léonard, *Les Angevins*, p. 77; Runciman, *Sicilian Vespers*, p. 115.

[28] Del Giudice, 'La famiglia', *ASPN*, v, 541–7; Dendias, 289–90.

to Egypt or, even stranger, that he turned up at the court of Edward II of England, are surely fanciful.[29]

Helena's mother, Theodora of Arta, died as a nun and a saint. She must often have thought of her daughter and grandchildren in Italy whom she had never seen. Her daughter Helena died as a martyr, persecuted not by infidels for her faith but by her menfolk for their own crass political and imperial ambitions. Helena's father Michael, the unscrupulous Despot of Epiros, might be accused of doing little to rescue her. Perhaps he never knew what befell her. For he died in 1267 when the news of Manfred's death may hardly have been known in Epiros and before Conradin, the last hope of the house of Hohenstaufen, had been killed at Tagliacozzo. Michael's heir was his eldest son Nikephoros. His daughter Thamar was, like Helena, to be sacrificed on the altar of diplomacy She too died in unhappy circumstances in Italy.

---

[29] Filangieri, *Registri*, IX, p. 262. Del Giudice, 'La famiglia', *ASPN*, v, 489–541; Dendias, 290–4. The figures of Manfred and his sons are depicted on the ambo of the cathedral at Bitonto.

———— ⬥⬥ ————

THAMAR, PRINCESS OF TARANTO,
1294–1309

THAMAR OR ITHAMAR was the second of the two daughters of Nikephoros Komnenos Doukas who succeeded his father Michael II as Despot of
Epiros in 1267. She was a niece of Helena, wife of Manfred of Sicily,
though they never met, and like Helena Thamar's life was to be dictated
by events in Italy across the water from her native land. Helena had
married the Hohenstaufen ruler in southern Italy and became Princess
of Taranto. Thamar married into the Angevin family which had dis-
placed the Hohenstaufen and became herself Princess of Taranto under
another flag. Her mother, Anna Palaiologina, was a niece of the
Emperor Michael VIII and devoted to the interests of the imperial
family that had come to power at Constantinople in 1261. She married
Nikephoros of Epiros in 1265, and for the next forty years exercised a
dominating influence on the policy of the Despotate of Epiros as its
basilissa or consort of the Despot. In the early years of their marriage she
persuaded her husband to temper his father's implacable hostility
towards the restored Empire of Constantinople. Her instincts and her
family ties with the house of Palaiologos led her to seek a peaceful
solution to the continuing independence from Constantinople of the
Principality over which she and her husband ruled as Despot and *basilissa*.[1]

The Byzantine historian George Pachymeres observes with approval
that the Despot Nikephoros had at first no territorial ambitions and was
content to live at peace with his neighbours.[2] Two events were to
disturb the peace between Epiros and Constantinople. The first was the

---

[1] On Anna, who was a Cantacuzene as well as a Palaiologina by birth, see D. M. Nicol,
The Byzantine Family of Kantakouzenos (Cantacuzenus) (Washington, D.C., 1968), no.
16. Western sources called her the Despina. Her correct title as wife of a Despot was
basilissa.

[2] George Pachymeres, *Relations historiques*, ed. A. Failler, II (Paris, 1984), iv. 26: p. 399.

defeat of Manfred of Sicily by Charles of Anjou at Benevento in 1266. The second was the enforcement of union with the Roman church by the Emperor Michael VIII. The two were connected. For it was to thwart Charles's ambition to reconquer Constantinople that the Emperor Michael offered to gratify the Pope by submitting the Ortho- dox church to the authority of Rome. In 1267, at the Pope's palace at Viterbo, a treaty was arranged among the western powers interested in a 'crusade' for the restoration of the Latin Empire of Constantinople. They were the dispossessed Latin Emperor Baldwin II, the French Prince of Achaia William of Villehardouin, and Charles of Anjou, King of Sicily. By terms of this treaty Charles became lord of all the territory in Epiros and Corfu which the late Manfred of Sicily had acquired through marriage to Helena. It was clear that Charles, as the Pope's choice to lead the proposed crusade, meant to make this territory his base for marching on Constantinople.

The Despot Nikephoros was in the same dilemma that had faced his father Michael of Epiros. He could either sacrifice his independence by joining forces with the Emperor in Constantinople against the threat from Italy, or he could throw in his lot with the invader. What per- suaded him to choose the latter course was the violent reaction in Byzantium against the Emperor's plan to win the favour of the Pope by offering to unite the Orthodox church under Rome. In 1274 the union of the churches was declared to have taken place at the Second Council of Lyons. The Emperor had won the first round. There would be no 'crusade' to displace him. The announcement of this diplomatic triumph, however, alienated thousands of his subjects who felt that their Orthodox faith had been betrayed. Many of the Emperor's own rela- tives turned against him. The *basilissa* Anna, wife of Nikephoros, and her mother Eulogia, the Emperor's sister, joined the opposition. Anna had tried to work for peace between her husband and her uncle, the Emperor in Constantinople. But she could not in conscience accept the union and she was shocked to hear that her mother had been exiled and imprisoned for opposing it. Anna joined her husband in denouncing the Emperor and in welcoming refugees from his persecution of the anti- unionists. The Despot Nikephoros, posing as the champion of Ortho- doxy, had no further qualms about allying himself with the Angevin rulers of Italy in the common cause of overthrowing the Emperor Michael. The fact that they too were heretics of the Roman faith did not deter him. They were born that way and could not help it. The crown of Constantinople which had eluded his father might yet be his if he rode to the city on the backs of his allies from Italy.

In 1277 he sent ambassadors across the water to begin discussions about a formal alliance between the Despotate of Epiros and the Angevin Kingdom of Naples and Sicily. Two years later Nikephoros swore homage to King Charles as his vassal and surrendered still more territory to add to what Charles was now pleased to call his Kingdom of Albania. Ambassadors from Naples were in Arta in April 1279 and there received the Despot's oath of homage and his signature to the draft of a treaty.[3] The alliance between Nikephoros and Charles of Anjou was never put to the test. Charles's anticipated crusade to Constantinople was driven off by the Byzantine army from Berat in Albania in April 1281. His attempt to launch a new armada by sea was thwarted by the revolution in Palermo known as the Sicilian Vespers in March 1282; and three years later, in January 1285, he died. By then the heretical Emperor Michael VIII was dead. The hated union of Lyons had been renounced and condemned by his son and successor, Andronikos II; and Nikephoros of Epiros could no longer stand on his high moral ground as the protector of Orthodoxy. But he was still not ready to sacrifice the independence of his principality by letting it become a mere province of the Byzantine Empire. His wife Anna felt that he was misguidedly obstinate.

For a few years after 1285 the alliance between Epiros and Naples was in abeyance. Charles II, the successor to the Angevin Kingdom, was held as a prisoner by the Aragonese. When he was released in 1289 he turned his mind to recreating and consolidating the colonial empire which his father had ruled. Sicily was lost, but he still claimed suzerainty over the French Principality of Achaia in the Peloponnese and over large stretches of Epiros and Albania. He could substantiate his claim by resurrecting his father's alliance with the Despot of Epiros, Nikephoros. It was Charles II who took the initiative, and it was well received. In June 1291 his envoys were in Arta to negotiate. They were empowered to propose that the alliance between Italy and Epiros could be strengthened by a bond of marriage. One of Charles's sons should marry one of the two daughters of Nikephoros and Anna.

Thirty-two years had passed since Manfred of Sicily had married Nikephoros's sister Helena. No one could pretend that her marriage had brought her much happiness. She was long since dead. But her extensive dowry in terms of territory was still owned by her late husband's successors, the Angevin Kings of Naples and Sicily. If Charles II were to marry one of Nikephoros's daughters the question of her dowry

[3] D. M. Nicol, 'The Relations of Charles of Anjou with Nikephoros of Epiros', *BF*, IV (1972), 170–94; Nicol, *The Despotate of Epiros*, II (Cambridge, 1984), pp. 18–24.

would need careful consideration. The negotiations went on for a long time. Meanwhile the issue was forced when the Emperor in Constantinople, Andronikos II, feeling that the time had come to bring the 'rebellious province' of Epiros to heel, launched an invasion by land and sea. It was not a success, and its failure encouraged the anti-imperialists in Epiros to continue to defy the government in Constantinople. The need to have a powerful ally across the water in Italy seemed more pressing than ever. This was the view of the Despot Nikephoros. His wife Anna was not of the same mind and there was, as a chronicler puts it, 'great tension' between husband and wife.[4]

In 1291 Charles II's envoys to Arta had suggested that one of Anna's daughters would be a suitable bride for one of his sons, either his third son Robert or his fourth son, Philip of Anjou. Her daughters were Maria and Thamar. Maria, the elder, put herself out of the running by marrying, or being kidnapped by, John Orsini, son of the so-called Count of the island of Cephalonia. In 1292–3 ambassadors went back and forth between Epiros and the court of Charles. In February 1294 Charles invested his fourth son Philip of Anjou with the title of Prince of Taranto and announced that he was to marry Thamar, the younger daughter of Nikephoros and Anna. The all-important question of Thamar's dowry had been resolved. The basic document for its resolution had been the text and substance of the dowry which Thamar's aunt Helena had brought to her husband Manfred in 1259. In addition Thamar was to provide Philip with an annual income of 100,000 hyperpyra and four castles in the south of Epiros, including the harbour of Lepanto (Naupaktos) and the fortress of Vonitza on the Ambracian Gulf, around the bay from Arta. In August 1294 Philip of Anjou, Prince of Taranto, was appointed by his father as suzerain over all the Angevin possessions in Greece, including the Principality of Achaia, the Duchy of Athens, the Kingdom of Albania, the island of Corfu and the properties on the coast of Epiros which had formerly belonged to Manfred. He was further invested with the grand title of Despot of Romania, meaning the whole of Latin-occupied Greece.

It seemed that the Despotate of Epiros, by stubbornly maintaining its independence from the Empire in Constantinople, was selling itself to the Angevin Kingdom of Naples and Sicily. Thamar's mother Anna had a plan to prevent this. She hoped that her daughter, instead of marrying a foreigner, should marry the heir-presumptive to the Byzan-

---

[4] Nicol, *Despotate of Epiros*, II, pp. 36–46. *Livre de la Conquête de la Princée de l'Amorée. Chronique de Morée*, ed. J. Longnon (Paris, 1911), c. 657, p. 262: 'si en fut grant division avec la despine sa femme'.

tine throne, Michael IX, son of Andronikos II. The young Michael was crowned as co-Emperor with his father in May 1294. If he took Thamar to wife the long separated and 'rebellious' province of Epiros might be reintegrated into the Byzantine Empire. This was Anna's hope and it was on this issue that she disagreed with her husband Nikephoros. At the eleventh hour she sent messengers to Constantinople to urge the benefits that would come from the union of Thamar and Michael IX. Her plea had no effect. The Emperor refused to consider it; and he had the support of the church. The Patriarch declared that the union would be uncanonical since the partners were related, however distantly, as cousins. Thamar's father must have been relieved; his own scheme for Thamar's marriage could go ahead without delay, and without 'tension' between himself and his wife.[5]

In July of the same year Philip of Taranto sent envoys of his own to Arta to complete the arrangements and draw up the necessary documents. His delegation was led by Roger, Archbishop of Santa Severina. It was he who had received the homage of the Despot Nikephoros to Charles I of Anjou in 1279. It was probably he also who, on the insistence of Thamar's mother, made Philip declare that he would respect his bride's Orthodox faith. In August 1294 he and his colleague Pierre de l'Isle escorted Thamar and her mother over to Italy. The wedding took place in that month at L'Aquila in the Abruzzi, which had been refounded by Philip's grandfather. The bride's mother may not have enjoyed the occasion very much. She would have preferred Thamar to have had a state wedding in Constantinople. At least she had done her husband's bidding, at whatever price. She stayed for a while in Italy to settle her daughter in and sailed back to Arta from Otranto with an escort of three galleys provided by Charles II.[6]

Among the wedding gifts which Thamar brought to her husband was a gold enamelled locket in the shape of an ivy leaf decorated with the fleur-de-lys of the house of Anjou and the double-headed eagle of Byzantium. It is now in the Archaeological Museum of Cividale del Friuli. It was a charming symbol of the union between the representatives of two cultures, of a symbiosis that proved to be no more substantial or permanent than a leaf in the wind. Early in 1295 Thamar went back to Epiros to visit her parents. Perhaps she had been summoned because of her father's ill-health. If so, it was a false alarm; for he

---

[5] A. E. Laiou, *Constantinople and the Latins. The foreign policy of Andronicus II, 1282–1328* (Cambridge, Mass., 1972), pp. 41–2 (cited below as Laiou, *Andronicus II*).

[6] Nicol, *Despotate of Epiros*, II, pp. 44–8.

lived for many months more. But he died at the end of 1296.[7] His widow Anna was then left alone to pay the price for his policy. Their only son Thomas, Thamar's brother, was heir to the Despotate. He had already been granted the title of Despot by the Emperor in Constantinople. But he was only six years old. Anna became regent of Epiros. Future policy with regard to Italy as well as to Constantinople was in her hands. She was, as a French chronicler describes her, 'one of the cleverest women in Romania'. But she knew that almost all of Romania or Greece was technically under the suzerainty of her son-in-law Philip of Taranto.[8]

In 1299 Philip was taken prisoner in war against Frederick II of Aragon and Sicily. He was in captivity for three years. Thamar waited anxiously for his release and did her best to raise the necessary ransom money. It is said that she pawned her golden and bejewelled coronet. She asked her mother Anna to contribute. Anna was glad to help and approached the Venetians, probably through their consul in Arta. They were polite but unco-operative. Anna did not care for being subservient to the Angevin masters of Epiros and Romania. But she had need of their help and she was sorry for her daughter Thamar. She did what she could to secure the release of Philip of Taranto. In 1302 the war between the Angevins and the Aragonese ended and Philip was set free by terms of the Treaty of Caltabellotta on 31 August of that year.[9]

Thamar got little thanks for all her efforts to get her husband back. It was bad enough that she had been obliged to change her name and to be called Caterina, Princess of Taranto. She also had cause to complain that Philip had not honoured his pledge to respect her Orthodox faith.[10] Her mother felt less and less inclined to accept the enforced subservience of her Despotate to the suzerainty of Philip of Taranto and his father. Once again she looked for help and comfort from her relatives in Constantinople. Her son Thomas, Thamar's brother, was growing up. She suggested that he might marry a daughter of the co-Emperor Michael IX whom she had once proposed as a more promising husband for Thamar. Anna would settle on Thomas and his wife the territory in Epiros which had constituted the dowry of Thamar, thereby rejecting outright the claims of Philip of Taranto. The Emperor Andronikos II had other problems on his mind. He showed little interest in Anna's

[7] D. M. Nicol, 'The date of the death of Nikephoros I of Epiros', *Rivista di Studi Bizantini e Slavi*, I (= *Miscellanea Agostino Pertusi*, I: Bologna, 1981), 251–7.

[8] *Livre de la Conquête* ed. Longnon, c. 974, p. 381.

[9] Nicol, *Despotate of Epiros*, II, pp. 50–2.

[10] Pachymeres, *De Andronico Palaeologo*, v. 30: II, p. 450 (*CSHB*).

proposal.[11] But Charles II and Philip were righteously indignant when they heard of her flagrant breach of contract. In 1304 Charles wrote to Anna at Arta to remind her of the exact terms of Thamar's marriage settlement. Her father Nikephoros being now dead, it was his widow's duty to hand over the Despotate to Philip of Taranto and make her son do homage to him. Thomas could then hold his inheritance as a fief of the Kingdom of Naples and Sicily. Anna's reply infuriated Charles, for she protested that the young Thomas could never do homage to the Prince of Taranto. Thomas's natural lord was the Emperor in Constantinople from whom he had acquired his title of Despot and the land that went with it. He was under no obligation to his brother-in-law Philip, who was certainly entitled to the four castles and the large annuity which had come to him as Thamar's dowry, but to no more. Anna was not entirely in the right. But she was defiant and not prepared to make concessions.[12]

Philip and his father, convinced of their rights under feudal law, saw that they would have to force her to concede. It would be a tiresome war but an easy one, since Anna was a mere woman and her son Thomas no more than fifteen years of age. They were proved wrong on both counts. The army that they sent to lay siege to Arta in 1304 was beaten off and Anna bribed its leaders to go home without trying a second time. In 1306 Philip of Taranto took charge of another attempt to humiliate the Despotate of Epiros. The Despot Thomas proved his manhood. Philip's army suffered heavy losses. He obliged Thomas to pay a large indemnity. But it was not the overwhelming and easy victory that he had expected; and in the autumn of 1306 Philip withdrew to Italy to lick his wounds.[13] There he unkindly vented his exasperation on Thamar, for he was convinced that she had been giving aid and support to her mother Anna and her brother Thomas behind his back. She had to pawn what was left of her jewellery to help pay for his campaigns in Epiros. A few years later he found a pretext for divorcing her. In 1309 Thamar was charged with adultery and made to confess that she had deceived her husband with at least forty of the leading lords of his court. The chief offender was the Count of Caserta, Bartolomeo Siginulfo, whom Charles II had appointed as Grand Chamberlain of his court only two years earlier. He was a married man and getting on in years. It was alleged that his wickedness was compounded by his implication in a plot to have Philip of Taranto assassinated. Some say that the

[11] In 1295 Michael IX had married an Armenian princess. Laiou, *Andronicus II*, pp. 54–6.
[12] Nicol, *Despotate of Epiros*, II, pp. 56–7.   [13] Ibid., pp. 57–61.

charges against him were never proved; others that he was tried and condemned on both counts in 1311.[14]

Thamar had no hope either of trial or of pardon. As an adulteress she was condemned by church and state. Her husband had every right to divorce her. It let him out of a marriage which was proving to be more and more troublesome. It left him free to find a more suitable wife. In 1313 he married Catherine of Valois, who had inherited the title of the long-defunct Latin Empire of Constantinople. Thamar, disgraced and divorced, was by then dead. She seems to have died as a nun, though whether praying for her estranged husband's soul or repenting of her own misdeeds is hard to say.[15] She had been Princess of Taranto for fifteen years, for three of which her husband had been a prisoner. She had produced five children for him, two sons and three daughters.[16] Years later, in 1328, Philip of Taranto tried to interest one of the sons, also called Philip, in reclaiming the land of his mother's birth for the Kingdom of Naples and Sicily and sent him off to Epiros with a fleet. The young Philip's heart was not in it. He got as far as Lepanto and there he died in 1331.[17] The rest of Thamar's children were brought up in Italy. They were not encouraged to recall their Greek origins nor to boast that they had in their veins the blood of the imperial Byzantine families of Cantacuzene and Palaiologos. The sons of their father's second marriage to Catherine of Valois were more promising material for the fulfilment of his ambitions; for they were heirs not only to the Principality of Taranto but also to the name if not the substance of the Latin Empire of Constantinople.

[14] The story of Thamar's adultery is told by Ptolemy of Lucca. *Ptolomaei Lucensis Historia Ecclesiastica*, ed. L. A. Muratori, *Rerum Italicarum Scriptores*, XI (Milan, 1727), col. 1232. See R. Caggese, *Roberto d'Angiò e i suoi tempi*, I (Florence, 1922), pp. 644–5. On Siginulfo, appointed Grand Chamberlain by Charles II in 1306–7, see R. Filangieri, *I Registri della Cancellaria Angioina*, XXXI (Naples, 1980), pp. 197, 198.

[15] The Aragonese version of the Chronicle of the Morea says nothing of Thamar's divorce, only that she died shortly after Philip's return from Greece, leaving two sons and three daughters. *Libro de los Fechos et Conquistas del Principado de la Morea*, ed. A. Morel-Fatio (Geneva, 1885), pp. 124–5. J. Longnon, *L'Empire latin de Constantinople et la principauté de Morée* (Paris, 1949), p. 302, says that in 1309 Philip repudiated her and put her in prison, where she died soon afterwards. Nicol, *Despotate of Epiros*, II, pp. 61–2.

[16] Thamar's children by Philip were two sons, Charles and Philip, and three daughters, Blanche, Jeanne and Beatrice. *Libro di los Fechos*, c. 569, p. 124. Charles was betrothed to Matilda, widow of Guy II Duke of Athens, but he died unmarried in 1315. Philip married first Beatrice of Bourbon-Clermont and then Violante of Aragon; he died in 1331. Blanche married Raymond Berengar, brother of Peter III of Aragon, and died in 1328. Jeanne married Ošin, King of Armenia. Beatrice married Walter II of Brienne in 1325. Caggese, *Roberto d'Angiò*, I, pp. 645–9; Longnon, *L'Empire latin*, p. 322; Nicol, *Despotate of Epiros*, II, p. 62 and note 114.

[17] Nicol, *Despotate of Epiros*, II, pp. 96–7.

Thamar, like Helena Doukaina before her, was the victim of her father's diplomatic manoeuvres. It was her forceful mother, the *basilissa* Anna Palaiologina, who had the last word in the battle of wits that she had fought with her husband. For in the end she succeeded in her plan to link the Despotate of Epiros more closely to the ruling family of Constantinople. About 1307, before Thamar's alleged misdemeanours, her son Thomas, who had refused to bow the knee to the Angevin rulers of Italy, married another Anna Palaiologina, the daughter of the co-Emperor Michael IX.[18] He remained as Despot in Epiros until 1318, when he was murdered by Nicholas Orsini of Cephalonia. He was the last direct descendant of the family of Komnenos Doukas who had created the Despotate of Epiros a hundred years before. In the city of Arta today the great church of the Virgin Paregoritissa stands as a lasting memorial to Thamar's parents. An inscription over its west door records their names as the Despot Nikephoros, Anna Palaiologina and their son the Despot. The Paregoritissa church was thus dedicated between 1294 and 1296, for their son Thomas was invested with the title of Despot in 1294 and Nikephoros died two years later. Could it have been for this important occasion that their daughter Thamar came back from Italy in 1295, so soon after her ill-starred marriage?[19]

---

[18] Nicol, *Despotate of Epiros*, II, p. 75; *PLP*, IX, no. 21344.
[19] D. M. Nicol, 'Thomas Despot of Epiros and the foundation date of the Paregoritissa at Arta', *Byzantina*, XIII, 2 (1985), 171–8.

CHAPTER THREE

———— ❧❧ ————

THEODORA RAOULAINA,
NUN AND SCHOLAR,
c. 1240–1300

ON 25 July 1261 a small expeditionary force of Byzantine troops entered Constantinople and drove out the Latin Emperor Baldwin II and his Venetian accomplices. The city had been in foreign hands for fifty-seven years, since the knights of the Fourth Crusade had conquered it and set up their Latin regime. Throughout those years a microcosm of the Byzantine Empire had survived and even prospered in exile with its capital at Nicaea in Asia Minor. The restoration of Constantinople had always been the dream and the hope of its rulers. In 1261 the Emperor at Nicaea was Michael VIII of the family of Palaiologos. He reigned as regent for and co-emperor with John Laskaris, the infant son of the late Emperor Theodore II. When in July the news was brought to him that his troops had suddenly entered Constantinople he refused to believe it. He was asleep in his camp near Nymphaion in Asia Minor about 200 miles away. His sister Eirene woke him with tactful gentleness by tickling his toes. He believed her story only when a courier arrived from Constantinople bringing the regalia of the wretched Latin Emperor Baldwin. Michael was then persuaded that God had worked a miracle.[1] Some weeks later, when he had made preparations for so grand an occasion, he entered Constantinople as Emperor of the Romans and was crowned as such by the Patriarch Arsenios. It was observed, however, that he was crowned alone. The boy Emperor John Laskaris, for whom he was supposed to be acting as regent, had been left behind in Nicaea. Word soon got around that he had been blinded and confined to a castle on the Black Sea coast. Michael Palaiologos thus became

---

[1] George Akropolites, *Historia. Georgii Acropolitae Opera*, ed. A. Heisenberg, I (Leipzig, 1903), pp. 183–4; George Pachymeres, *Relations historiques*, ed. A. Failler, II (Paris, 1984), pp. 206–7. On the early career of Michael Palaiologos, see D. J. Geanakoplos, *Emperor Michael Palaeologus and the West 1258–1282* (Cambridge, Mass., 1959), pp. 16–115; D. M. Nicol, *The Last Centuries of Byzantium, 1261–1453*, 2nd ed. (Cambridge, 1993), pp. 29–37.

sole ruler of the restored Byzantine Empire, his reign founded on a crime.

The Patriarch Arsenios who had performed his coronation excommunicated him. Michael soon found a pretext for dismissing Arsenios and appointing a substitute who was prepared to receive him back into the church. He was Joseph, abbot of a monastery near Ephesos. Church and society were at once divided between the Arsenites, who refused to accept the new Patriarch and remained loyal to the name and the memory of his wronged predecessor, and the Josephites, who accepted the change. The schism in the Byzantine church was aggravated by the new Emperor's determination to announce and enforce union with the church of Rome. Arsenites and Josephites joined forces in condemning and resisting it. The Emperor's favourite sister Eirene, who had woken him to the glad news of his triumph, turned against him. Her husband, John Cantacuzene, had died about 1258. As was the fashion among aristocratic widows in Byzantium she became a nun, taking the monastic name of Eulogia. She had four daughters: Theodora, Anna, Maria and Eugenia. Theodora and Anna at least inherited their mother's virtues of piety and independent spirit; and they were proud to bear their father's name of Cantacuzene, for he had been Grand Domestic or commander-in-chief of the army in Nicaea.[2]

It is with Theodora that the present study is concerned. She was born about 1240 in the Empire of Nicaea during the years of exile.[3] In 1256 she married George Mouzalon, a man of undistinguished birth who had risen to the rank of *protovestiarios*. Her marriage was arranged by the Emperor Theodore II, whose policy it was to raise novi homines to positions of power and influence.[4] When Theodore died in 1258 Mouzalon was the first to assume the regency for the young heir apparent John IV. This was not to the taste of the older aristocracy whom the late Emperor had slighted or ignored, among them Michael Palaiologos. The army, especially the foreign mercenaries whom Michael commanded, took the law into their own hands. They had their own grievances against the late Emperor. At the memorial service for him only nine days after his death, the troops broke into the church at Sosandra near Magnesia and massacred all the members of the Mouzalon family

---

[2] The career of Eirene-Eulogia Palaiologina is summarised in *PLP*, ix, no. 21360.

[3] Previous biographical notices of Theodora include: A. Ch. Chatzes, Οἱ Ῥαοὺλ, Ῥάλ, Ῥάλαι (*1080–1800*) (Kirchhain, 1909), no. 8; Sp. P. Lambros, Δύο Ἑλληνίδες βιβλιογράφοι, *NE*, x (1913), 347–8; D. M. Nicol, *The Byzantine Family of Kantakouzenos (Cantacuzenus)* (Washington, D. C., 1968), no. 14; S. Fassoulakis, *The Byzantine Family of Raoul Ra(l)es* (Athens, 1973), no. 11; *PLP*, v, no. 10943.

[4] Pachymeres, ed. Failler, I, p. 41.

that they could find. The church and the altar ran with blood. The congregation fled in panic. 'Ladies of quality and matrons', who had been there to pay their respects, joined the stampede for the doors. The service was abandoned. No one seemed able or willing to put a stop to the fury of the soldiers. Only one voice was heard protesting at their savagery and calling for a halt to the massacre. It was the voice of Theodora, the wife of the *protovestiarios* George Mouzalon. Her uncle Michael Palaiologos loudly and firmly reproved her and ordered her to keep quiet for fear that she herself might be cut down.[5] He was the one man who could perhaps have commanded the troops to desist. It is hard not to suspect that he had his reasons for allowing them a free hand. When order was restored Theodora's husband was dead and his place as regent of the Empire was taken by her uncle Michael. The massacre of the Mouzalon family could never be directly attributable to him. But it was his first step to the throne.

Once installed and properly crowned as Emperor in Constantinople Michael VIII published an honours list rewarding those who had supported him. Among those honoured was one John Raoul. He was given the rank and title of *protovestiarios* which his father had once held and of which the unhappy Mouzalon had been deprived by death. It was the Emperor's wish that John Raoul should marry Mouzalon's widow Theodora.[6] For her it was a better match than her first marriage which had also been arranged with or without her consent. Theodora had a strong sense of social class. By marrying John Raoul she became doubly entitled to style herself *protovestiarissa*, which she did for the rest of her life. She also added her new husband's name to the list of her surnames and was proud thereafter to be known as Theodora Cantacuzene Palaiologina Raoulaina. It was an honourable addition. The family of Raoul had a greater claim to ancestral nobility than the upstart house of Mouzalon; and Theodora was not alone among the 'ladies of quality and matrons' of Byzantine society in the thirteenth century in being a snob. In times past empresses and princesses in Constantinople had been content to be known simply by the surnames of their husbands. In Theodora's day they were fond of qualifying themselves with long lists of family names which they had acquired by marriage or by affinity. The practice advertised their solidarity with the *eugeneis* or golden line of the ruling class, as Pachymeres described them.[7] Theodora sometimes described herself with the grand title of 'Theodora, niece of the

[5] Pachymeres, ed. Failler, I, pp. 63–89. Geanakoplos, *Emperor Michael*, pp. 33–46.
[6] Pachymeres, ed. Failler, I, pp. 153–5.
[7] Pachymeres, ed. Failler, I, p. 93.

Emperor of the Romans, Theodora of the families of Cantacuzene, Angelos, Doukas, Komnenos, Palaiologos, and wife of John Raoul Doukas Komnenos the *protovestiarios*.' It is significant that she never felt impelled to advertise her brief connexion with the family of her first husband. The Mouzalones had little claim to fame or nobility, for all that they had produced a rather ineffectual Patriarch of Constantinople in the twelfth century.[8]

Her second husband John Raoul served the Emperor Michael as an officer in the campaigns in northern Greece to reincorporate into the Empire the rebellious provinces of Epiros and Thessaly, whose rulers fought for their independence from the new regime in Constantinople. He was proud of his own aristocratic birth, boasting affinity with the families of Komnenos, Angelos and Doukas. His ancestors of the Raoul family, however, had been Normans from the south of Italy who settled in Greece in the twelfth century and became fully integrated into Byzantine society, adopting the Orthodox faith and marrying Byzantine ladies. John was also connected with the family of Petraliphas, another hellenised Norman family from Italy. His marriage to Theodora, which took place probably in 1261, ended with his death about 1274. She had at least two daughters by him, Eirene Raoulaina named after her grandmother, and Anna. The Rhetor or orator of the Great Church of Constantinople, Manuel Holobolos, wrote a letter of consolation to Theodora on the death of her husband. It was perhaps as well that he died when he did. For it was after the year 1274 that his wife fell foul of her uncle the Emperor Michael and was disgraced.[9]

It was the year in which the Emperor's policy of union with the Roman church bore fruit in the decree of union pronounced at the Second Council of Lyons. The Pope was delighted. The Emperor was satisfied. It remained for him to persuade his people and his church that he had done the right thing. This proved to be more difficult than he had supposed. The Orthodox were deeply offended by what they saw as a betrayal of their inherited faith. Opposition to the union was loud and strong among the laity as well as the clergy. A leading figure in the protest was the Emperor's own sister, by then the nun Eulogia, the mother of Theodora. Mother and daughter were very close. As soon as

---

[8] Nicholas IV Mouzalon was Patriarch of Constantinople from 1147 to 1151.

[9] Manuel Holobolos, *Letter* to Theodora Palaiologina Raoulaina in A. Papadopoulos-Kerameus, Ἱεροσολυμιτικὴ Βιβλιοθήκη, I (St Petersburg, 1891), p. 345. On John Raoul and his daughters by Theodora, see Fassoulakis, *Byzantine Family of Raoul*, nos. 6, 14, 15. On the origins of the families of Raoul and Petraliphas, see D. M. Nicol, 'Symbiosis and integration. Some Greco-Latin families in Byzantium in the 11th to 13th centuries', *BF*, VII (1979), 113–55 (= Nicol, *Collected Studies*, II (London, 1986), no. III).

her husband died Theodora followed Eulogia's example and became a nun.[10] Together the two pious ladies stirred up the opposition to the Emperor's unionist policy in Constantinople and beyond. From the seclusion of her convent Eulogia organised a cabal against the misguided Emperor who had once been her favourite brother. Two of her daughters lived beyond the reach of his displeasure. Maria had settled in Bulgaria as the wife of its Tsar. Anna lived in Epiros as the wife of its independent Despot who had other reasons for opposing the Emperor Michael. Both worked as willing agents of their mother's anti-unionist propaganda. Both helped the cause by denouncing the Emperor and his few supporters as heretics and by giving asylum to refugees from his persecution of those whom he counted as dissidents. Theodora was among them, backing her mother's campaign from the centre of opposition in Constantinople.[11]

Many grim tales are told of the Emperor Michael's reign of terror. When persuasion failed he and his agents turned to threatening, imprisoning and persecuting his opponents. Martyrs for the true and Orthodox faith were created, some of whom are commemorated as Confessors to this day. Among the victims were Theodora's brothers-in-law, Isaac and Manuel Raoul. Both were imprisoned for their defiance and blinded on the Emperor's orders when they refused to recant. Theodora and her mother, denounced as ringleaders of the dissenters, were arrested, banished from Constantinople and locked up in the fortress of St Gregory on the Black Sea coast.[12] There they languished until the storm was over and the Orthodox faith uncontaminated by Roman doctrines was restored. The Emperor was anxious to keep the Popes informed about the difficulties that he was facing in enforcing the union of the churches. In 1278 he sent a report to Pope Nicholas III by hand of a western messenger who had seen for himself the strength of the opposition in Constantinople. The report, written in Latin, lists the troublemakers whom the Emperor had felt obliged to chastise, imprison or mutilate. Many of the offenders were of the imperial family. Among those named were Isaac and Manuel Raoul, the brothers of John, the late husband of Theodora, as well as the Emperor's

---

[10] The monastic name Kyriake sometimes attributed to her derives from a misreading of the manuscript notice recording her death. See below, note 37.

[11] D. M. Nicol, 'The Byzantine reaction to the Second Council of Lyons, 1274', *Studies in Church History*, VII, ed. C. J. Cuming and D. Baker (Cambridge, 1971), 130 (= Nicol, *Collected Studies*, I (London, 1972), no. VI).

[12] Pachymeres, *De Andronico Palaeologo*, II, p. 15 (*CSHB*). On Isaac and Manuel Raoul, see Fassoulakis, *Byzantine Family of Raoul*, nos. 7, 8. Nicol 'The Byzantine Reaction', 131–2.

own sister and her daughters, namely Eulogia and particularly Theodora. They, along with other 'baronesses', had been incarcerated and all their property movable and immovable had been confiscated by the treasury.[13]

The union of Lyons proclaimed in 1274 served its purpose for a few years. It saved Byzantium from its western enemies who were set on winning back the prize of Constantinople which they had lost in 1261. Such had been the Emperor Michael's intention in offering a reunion of Christendom on the Pope's terms. But the Popes themselves began to see that the union was a sham and a political gambit. In 1281 Pope Martin IV excommunicated the Emperor Michael and so rendered the union meaningless. In the same year the threat of another Fourth Crusade became a reality. It was thwarted before it had got much further than Sicily. A few months later Michael VIII died, in December 1282. With him died the last pretence that the union of the churches could ever be achieved by force. As soon as he was gone, his son and successor Andronikos II Palaiologos declared that it was over. Those whom his father had victimised for protesting against it at once became the heroes of the hour. Theodora and her mother Eulogia were set free and hurried back to Constantinople. The Patriarch Joseph was restored to his throne. Eulogia, we are told, was most insistent that the new Emperor, who was her nephew, must issue a public statement of his renunciation of the union with Rome; and she persuaded the dowager Empress and widow of the late Michael VIII that it was idle to pray for the salvation of her husband's soul.[14] The bishops who had held fast to the Orthodox faith met in Constantinople in January 1283 to condemn the Patriarch John Bekkos who had done his Emperor's bidding by supporting the union. Orthodoxy in its most intolerant form was restored, shorn of the errors and heresies of the Roman church. But the effort proved too much for the Patriarch Joseph. He was elderly and infirm. He resigned in March 1283 and died a few weeks later. A new Patriarch had to be found.

The fanatical Orthodox had been appeased by the renunciation of the union with Rome. The Arsenites, however, were not satisfied. They too had been persecuted by the late Emperor Michael. They had never

---

[13] R.-J. Loenertz, 'Mémoire d'Ogier, protonotaire, pour Marco et Marchetto nonces de Michel VIII Paléologue auprès du Pape Nicholas III. 1278 printemps-été', OCP, XXXI (1965), 374–408; D. M. Nicol, 'The Greeks and the union of the Churches: The report of Ogerius, protonotarius of Michael VIII Palaiologos', in Nicol, Collected Studies, I, no. VII.

[14] Pachymeres, De Andronico Palaeologo, II, pp. 14–15, 17–19 (CSHB); Nikephoros Gregoras, History. Byzantina Historia, ed. L. Schopen, I, p. 160 (CSHB).

acknowledged Joseph as Patriarch. Now that he was gone they hoped to see one of their own installed as the true successor of the Patriarch Arsenios. They were disappointed when the new Emperor Andronikos selected a man of letters and learning, George of Cyprus. He was neither a monk nor a fanatic; and it was said that, on theological grounds, he had been suspected of unionist tendencies. On his elevation to the Patriarchate he assumed the name of Gregory II. The Arsenites determined to make life as difficult as possible for him. Theodora, though at heart an Arsenite, was more moderate and tolerant than many of her hot-headed friends; and she admired Gregory of Cyprus for his scholarship, a taste which she fully shared and which he may have implanted in her. In later years Gregory was to become her spiritual father and her close friend and companion in collecting and exchanging manuscripts of classical Greek authors. On grounds of conscience, however, Theodora remained loyal to the memory of the Patriarch Arsenios.[15]

Early in 1284 the Emperor Andronikos made a special effort to bring peace to the Orthodox church by summoning a gathering of bishops, clergy and laymen of both persuasions to resolve their differences. They met during Holy Week at Adramyttion on the coast of Asia Minor. Theodora and her mother Eulogia were there, as well as her sister Anna of Epiros who had come all the way to Constantinople when she heard the glad news of her mother's release and the end of the union. Theodora and her mother attended as friends of the new Patriarch Gregory and perhaps they had hopes of bringing some reason to bear on the fanaticism of the Arsenites. In this they failed. The gathering at Adramyttion, despite an appeal for a divine miracle, came to no agreement and no conclusion. The storm of the Arsenite schism was only temporarily calmed. The Emperor made one more extraordinary gesture to pour oil on the waters. He allowed the Arsenites to have the body of their heroic martyr transferred from its place of exile to Constantinople. A great fuss was made of the occasion. The mortal remains of Arsenios were received at the gates of the city by the Patriarch Gregory and the Emperor and carried in torchlight procession to lie in the cathedral of St Sophia.[16]

---

[15] On George (Gregory) of Cyprus, see A. Papadakis, *Crisis in Byzantium. The* Filioque *Controversy in the Patriarchate of Gregory II of Cyprus (1283–1289)* (New York, 1983).

[16] Pachymeres, *De Andronico Palaeologo*, II, p. 69 (*CSHB*); Gregoras, I, p. 167 (*CSHB*). V. Laurent, *Les régestes des actes des patriarches de Constantinople*, I: *Les actes des patriarches*, fasc. IV (Paris, 1971), no. 1470. On the canonisation of the Patriarch Arsenios, see Ruth Macrides, 'Saints and sainthood in the early Palaiologan period', in *The Byzantine Saint*, ed. S. Hackel (University of Birmingham 14th Spring Symposium of

Theodora and her sister Anna seem to have gone back to Constantinople after Easter 1284. Their mother Eulogia as well as the Patriarch Gregory stayed on in Adramyttion. It was there, later in the year, that Eulogia died. Her daughters came back in time for her funeral. The Patriarch, who had been recalled to the capital in December, hoped to see them on their journey at the port at Gallipoli. They travelled by a different route, however, and he wrote to them lamenting their loss and saying how sad he was that their paths had not crossed.[17] It was probably after her mother's death that Theodora sought and obtained the Emperor's permission to restore a monastery church and buildings in Constantinople. Her private property had by then been given back to her and she used it for this pious purpose. It was an ancient foundation that had fallen into ruins and it was dedicated to St Andrew of Crete. It stood in the district of the city known as Krisis. Theodora came to be known as its second founder. She transformed it into a convent of nuns and it was there that she lived and prayed and studied for the rest of her life. The court poet Manuel or Maximos Planoudes, who knew her well and admired her learning, wrote three epigrams in heroic couplets on the church of St Andrew in Krisei built by his friend the *protovestiaria* Theodora Cantacuzene Palaiologina Komnene Raoulaina. He praised her especially for her steadfast adherence to the Orthodox faith for which, as he says, she had suffered much. Before long the Emperor allowed her to build a shrine in her convent to commemorate the saintly Patriarch Arsenios and his mortal remains were transferred there from St Sophia. Such gestures, though politically risky, were meant to placate the fanatical Arsenites. But they were to remain in schism from the established church for another twenty-five years.[18]

It was in the tranquillity of her convent of St Andrew that Theodora at last felt free to indulge her love of learning and literature. The world and the turmoil in the church had been too much with her. After about 1285 she seems to have decided to divide her time between her monastic duties and her scholarly life. Her daughters had by then married, one of

Byzantine Studies: Studies supplementary to *Sobornost*, v (1981), 67–87, especially 73–9).

[17] Gregory of Cyprus, *Letters*, ed. S. Eustratiades, *EPh*, IV (1909), no. ρνη′, pp. 116–18; Laurent, *Régestes*, IV, no. 1477.

[18] Pachymeres, *De Andronico Palaeologo*, II, pp. 85–6 (*CSHB*). Maximos Planoudes, *Epigrams*, ed. Sp. P. Lambros, *NE*, XIII (1916), 414–21. On St Andrew in Krisei: R. Janin, *La géographie ecclésiastique de l'empire byzantin*, I: *Le siège de Constantinople et le patriarcat oecuménique*; III: *Les églises et les monastères*, 2nd ed. (Paris, 1969), pp. 32–5. V. Laurent, 'Les grandes crises religieuses à Byzance. La fin du schisme arsénite', *Académie roumaine. Bulletin de la section historique*, XXVI (1945), 225–313.

them to a brother of the Emperor Andronikos.[19] She had the time, the money and the inclination to acquire a library of her own and to exchange books and ideas with other scholars. Byzantine ladies with a taste for learning were rare but not unknown. Theodora Raoulaina, however, was unique in the society of her time. In default of her own testimony, there is no indication of where, how, or by whom she was educated. It is possible that she learnt most from her learned friend Gregory of Cyprus. Her knowledge of classical Greek literature was prodigious and her interest in it must have been stimulated by private tuition from an early age. All the scholars and intellectuals whom she gathered around her or with whom she corresponded were men. They were the luminaries of the revival of classical Greek studies in Constantinople in the late thirteenth century, rediscovering and re-editing lost or neglected manuscripts of antiquity. Many in the monastic world objected that the study of such secular and pagan, or Hellenic, literature was none of the business of a monk or a nun. Theodora did not take this view. Nor did her friend, correspondent and collaborator Maximos Planoudes, who was himself a monk and at the same time a teacher and scholar with an extraordinary range of knowledge. Planoudes was also one of the very few scholars of his age to master Latin and to translate Latin texts into Greek. Theodora seems to have known no Latin. But she consulted Planoudes about copies of Greek manuscripts.

Unfortunately, none of her own letters to her friends has been preserved, although Planoudes and others complimented her on her epistolary style. Correspondence between Byzantine intellectuals was often more concerned with the display of erudition and style than with the conveying of information. In one of his letters to Theodora, however, Planoudes demonstrates the scope of her scholarly interests. He refers to a book about harmonics which she had in her collection and which she hoped that he might emend and compare with his own copy of the same manuscript. He laments the fact that his copy is missing, since he lent it to one Autoreianos who then left Constantinople taking it with him. Planoudes rather hoped that Theodora might use her influence with Autoreianos to get the manuscript back. In this and other letters Planoudes refers to Theodora as her 'ladyship'. This was more than deferential and rhetorical courtesy due to an aristocratic lady. For Theodora was his patroness and benefactress. In his epigrams Planoudes carefully expounds her noble genealogy, extols her sufferings for the cause

[19] Eirene Raoulaina Palaiologina married Constantine Palaiologos. *PLP*, x, no. 24142. Theodora may also have been the mother of Anna Komnene Raoulaina Strategopoulina. Fassoulakis, *Byzantine Family of Raoul*, nos. 14, 15.

of the Orthodox faith, and describes her as the most learned among women. Hypocrisy and flattery were part of the stock in trade of letters to one's patron. But in this case Planoudes surely spoke the truth. For Theodora was extremely well connected; she had been a victim of religious bigotry; and she was without doubt the most erudite woman of her day.[20]

She picked the brains of many other learned men and sought their advice on numerous manuscripts that came her way. Constantine Akropolites, who inherited wealth as well as books from his learned father George, freely gave her his opinion on a copy of a mathematical treatise which she sent to him for appraisal. His opinion of it was not high. He too addressed Theodora as his most noble and learned lady.[21] Another of her scholarly friends was Manuel Holobolos, the monk Maximos. He too had suffered cruel punishment and exile for his religious convictions. He too came back to Constantinople in 1283 and was reinstated in his former post as teacher of rhetoric in the Patriarchal School. For all his stand against union with the Roman church, Holobolos shared with Planoudes the rare distinction of being a Latin scholar as well as an editor of Greek texts. He translated some works of Boethius and wrote scholia on Aristotle and Theocritus. There is no evidence that he corresponded with Theodora. But the fact that he knew her family well may be inferred from the letter of condolence which he wrote to her on the occasion of the death of her second husband about 1274.[22]

The leading lights of what were to her the younger generation of Byzantine scholars were less familiar to her. She seems to have had no dealings with Theodore Metochites, the greatest polymath of the fourteenth century. His political, academic and social rival Nikephoros Choumnos certainly corresponded with her. She knew that he was an expert on the text of Aristotle. From one of his letters to her we know that Theodora asked Choumnos if she might borrow his copy of a manuscript of Aristotle's *Meteorologica* with the Commentaries of Alexander of Aphrodisias. Theodora had a winning way, and no doubt Choumnos, a younger man, was flattered by the attentions of so distinguished a lady. He lent her his manuscript, though it almost broke his

---

[20] Maximos Planoudes, *Letters*, ed. M. Treu, *Maximi monachi Planudis epistulae* (Breslau, 1890), no. LXIIX, pp. 85–7, 230, 245–7. S. Kugéas, 'Zur Geschichte der Münchener Thukydideshandschrift Augustanus F', *BZ*, XVI (1907), 601–2.

[21] C. Constantinides, *Higher Education in Byzantium in the Thirteenth and Early Fourteenth Centuries (1204 – ca. 1310)* (Nicosia, 1982), Appendix, p. 164, no. 60.

[22] M. Treu, 'Manuel Holobolos', *BZ*, V (1906), 538–9; Constantinides, *Higher Education*, pp. 50–9; *PLP*, IX, no. 21047. For Holobolos's letter to Theodora (unpublished), see above, note 9.

heart to do so. He praised her as the wisest and most discerning lady; and, knowing that she had an eye for the quality and beauty of manuscripts he apologised for the poor and uncultured calligraphy of his copy.[23]

The most influential of Theodora's learned friends was George of Cyprus who was Patriarch as Gregory II from 1283 to 1289. As already mentioned, he wrote as a sorrowing friend of the family to console her when her mother died in 1284. Nearly thirty more of his letters to Theodora exist, only three of which have been published in full.[24] Gregory was her father confessor as well as sharing and nurturing her enthusiasm for classical scholarship. He addressed her not as his 'lady' but as his only child, his daughter. He prayed that God would multiply her wisdom and learning and that she would be seen and known to be superior to women of the past in her pursuit of literary education. He claimed that her library was bigger than his own. They corresponded like ardent bibliophiles about bindings, about manuscripts of Demosthenes, of Aristeides and of the ethical works of St Basil the Great. Theodora once asked him to commission his own scribe Melitas to make her a copy of Demosthenes and to take care not to blemish it with blots or stains. Gregory was quite willing to do this in due course, when after Easter people took to eating meat again and there were more skins available for making parchment. Lent was a bad time for finding writing material. But he was a little aggrieved that she gave instructions to his scribe; for Melitas was a professional and a careful master of his art, all of whose work was immaculate.[25]

Gregory of Cyprus was one of the most learned men of his age in theology as well as in classical scholarship. It was his theological erudition that led to his downfall. In 1285 he issued a document (*Tomos*) in which he tried to define more clearly the Orthodox doctrine of the Trinity in a manner that might be less offensive to Christians of the Roman church. Some bishops thought his definition to be heretical.

---

[23] Nikephoros Choumnos, *Letters*, ed. J. F. Boissonade, *Anecdota nova* (Paris, 1844), nos. 76, 77, pp. 91–3. J. Verpeaux, *Nicéphore Choumnos, homme d'état et humaniste byzantin (ca 1250/1255–1327)* (Paris, 1959), pp. 54, 67, 73–4; P. M. L. Leone, 'Le epistole di Niceforo Chumno nel cod. Ambros. gr. C 71 sup.', *EEBS*, xxxix–xl (1972–3), 75–95.

[24] W. Lameere, *La tradition manuscrite de la correspondance de Grégoire de Chypre, patriarche de Constantinople (1283–1289)* (Brussels–Rome, 1937), pp. 150–61. Substantial extracts of Gregory's letters to Theodora are printed in Kugéas, 'Zur Geschichte', 595–600. See also Planoudes, ed. Treu, *Planudes*, p. 261.

[25] Gregory of Cyprus, *Letters*, ed. S. Eustratiades, *EPh*, v (1910), no. ρπζ', pp. 450–2 (pp. 197–9 in the Alexandria edition); Laurent, *Les régestes*, iv, no. 1547. N.G. Wilson, 'Books and readers in Byzantium', *Byzantine Books and Bookmen* (Washington, D.C., 1975), p. 2.

Gregory was forced to resign.[26] He retired to the monastery of the Virgin Hodegetria in Constantinople. He wrote to Theodora complaining about his new quarters there which, aside from other defects, housed an army of mice. Theodora took pity on him and invited him to make his monastic cell in a little house called Aristine which she had renovated alongside her own convent of St Andrew. There her friend and comforter died after a long illness in 1289. His theological adventure into the nature of the Trinity had by then caused such a contentious fuss that the Emperor feared public demonstrations if Gregory were given a funeral proper for a former Patriarch. Theodora had wanted to bury her friend with fitting ceremony. She was expressly forbidden to do so.[27]

Although none of Theodora's own letters to which her many correspondents refer has yet come to light, some of her other writings have survived. Particularly interesting and poignant is her Life of the ninth-century saints Theodore and Theophanes.[28] Hagiography was one of the recognised forms of literary exercise among Byzantine intellectuals. Saints' lives provided improving reading as well as a medium for advertising a writer's style and erudition. Theodora, however, obviously selected for her subject the brothers Theodore and Theophanes because their fate was tragically evocative of that of her own relatives. They had been cruelly persecuted by the Emperor Theophilos because of their refusal to accept the edict of iconoclasm. They were beaten and branded on the forehead with twelve verses declaring that they were heretics. They became known as the Graptoi.[29] Theodora herself had been persecuted for her outspoken defence of what she believed to be the truth. The two martyrs for the same cause in her own family were her brothers-in-law Isaac and Manuel Raoul, who had been blinded and thrown into prison. It would have been against literary convention to name them. She makes only one oblique mention of the comparable religious turmoil of her own day and the victimisation of those who, like the Graptoi, steadfastly refused to do their Emperor's bidding in a matter of conscience. Her Life of Theophanes the Confessor and his brother Theodore is the only known original work written by Theo-

---

[26] Papadakis, Crisis in Byzantium, pp. 79f, 132f.

[27] Gregoras, I, pp. 178–9 (CSHB); Pachymeres, De Andronico Palaeologo, II, pp. 131–52 (CSHB). Letter of Gregory (extract) in Kugéas, 'Zur Geschichte', 600. On the monydrion of Aristine: Janin, La géographie ecclésiastique, pp. 56–7.

[28] Ed. A. Papadopoulos-Kerameus, Ἀνάλεκτα Ἰεροσολυμιτικῆς Σταχυολογίας, IV (St Petersburg, 1897), pp. 185–223; V, pp. 397–9.

[29] See W. Treadgold, The Byzantine Revival 780–842 (Stanford, Calif., 1988), pp. 310–11.

dora. It was a work of piety but also a vehicle for demonstrating her wide reading of classical Greek authors. She quotes not only from the Scriptures but also from Hesiod, Homer, Diogenes Laertius, Dionysios of Halicarnassos, Euripides and Strabo. No wonder that her erudition was so much admired.[30]

Her love of books extended to a love of illustrations for them and of calligraphy. At least two manuscripts are known which were written by her own hand. One is a copy of the Orations of Aelius Aristeides in the Vatican Library consisting of 425 folios (Cod. Vat. gr. 1899).[31] Aristeides, the Greek rhetorician of the second century AD, was a great favourite with Byzantine scholars as a stylist and exemplar of acceptable Greek prose. The manuscript, clearly an autograph, is prefaced by an eight-line dedication in octosyllabic verse explaining that it is the book of Aristeides 'copied to the highest degree of accuracy by Theodora, the child of the sister of the Emperor of New Rome, and a Cantacuzene related to the imperial families of Angelos, Doukas and Palaiologos, and the wife of the *protovestiarios* John Raoul Doukas Komnenos'. The dedication may be by another hand, but the text is written by Theodora herself. The reference to the Emperor as her uncle must refer to Michael VIII who died in 1282. The reference to her husband John Raoul dates the manuscript to before 1274, the approximate year of his death. She must have written it in happier times, before she became a nun and before she was exiled from Constantinople. The other known autograph manuscript of Theodora is a copy of the Commentary of Simplicius on the *Physics* of Aristotle now in the Historical Museum in Moscow.[32] This too is prefaced by an eight-line dedication in verse naming the calligraphist of the text as 'the niece of the Emperor, the gift of God [Theodora], of the families of Doukas, Komnenos, Palaiologos, the wife of John Raoul'. This too she must have copied before 1274. Assuming that she was born about 1240, she must have transcribed both these manuscripts when in her thirties and still happily married.

Later in her life, after she came back to Constantinople from exile and set herself up in her convent of St Andrew, she added to her already extensive library but she also endowed an atelier of scribes and artists under her patronage. A group of (at least) fifteen exquisitely written Gospels, Lectionaries and Psalters with striking portraits of the Evange-

[30] Ed. Papadopoulos-Kerameus, pp. 190, 192, 196, 197, 202, 204, 205, 207, 208, 211.

[31] A. Turyn, *Codices Graeci Vaticani Saeculis XIII et XIV scripti annorumque notis instructi* (Vatican City, 1964), pp. 63–5 and plates 36 and 168c.

[32] B. L. Fonkić, 'Zametki o grečeskich rukopisjach Sovietskich chranilišč', *VV*, xxxvi (1974), 134.

lists has been attributed to the scriptorium and workshop founded and financed by Theodora. The monogram 'Palaiologina' at the head of two of the Canon Tables in this group of manuscripts seems to confirm its association with her, even though she usually preferred to sign herself as Cantacuzene or Raoulaina.[33] It is likely that yet another Lectionary produced by the same team of calligraphers and illuminators can now be identified.[34] These were sumptuous works of art rather than of scholarship. They demonstrate in a vivid manner Theodora's aesthetic taste, the complement to her love of the more arid manifestations of scholarship.

Shortly before her death Theodora presented a manuscript from her library to the monastery of St Athanasios, the Great Lavra, on Mount Athos. The manuscript, now in Paris, contains the Commentaries on the Four Gospels by Theophylact of Ochrida, the learned Archbishop of Bulgaria in the late eleventh century.[35] It is possible that the manuscript had once been in the library of Gregory of Cyprus who admired the works of Theophylact. Theodora's last recorded act reveals her not as a lover of art, literature and scholarship, nor as a cloistered nun, but as a woman of action playing her part in public affairs. In 1295 Alexios Philanthropenos, a soldier who had been highly successful in battle against the Turks in western Asia Minor, was hailed as Emperor by his jubilant troops, supported by the local Greek inhabitants who had for long felt neglected by the Emperors in Constantinople. Theodora was distantly related to Philanthropenos, as was the Emperor Andronikos II. It was he who commissioned her to go to Asia Minor and reason with the rebel. Theodora took with her her brother-in-law, Isaac Raoul, who had been blinded for his own subversive activities. Perhaps he was to serve as a warning. For Philanthropenos must have known that the

---

[33] H. Belting, *Das illuminierte Buch in der spätbyzantinischen Gesellschaft* (Heidelberg, 1970), pp. 57, 66–7; H. Buchthal and H. Belting, *Patronage in Thirteenth-Century Constantinople. An atelier of Late Byzantine book illumination and calligraphy* (Dumbarton Oaks Studies XVI: Washington, D. C., 1978), pp. 6, 100 and plate 19.

[34] Kathleen Maxwell, 'Another lectionary of the "atelier" of the Palaiologina, Vat. Gr. 532', *DOP*, XXXVII (1983), 47–54; H. Hunger, *Schreiben und Lesen in Byzanz. Die byzantinische Buchkultur* (Munich, 1989), pp. 49, 90, 131. Another manuscript belonging to the same group may be the Gospel Lectionary of the late thirteenth century in the National Library of Athens (Cod. 2546). It comes from the monastery of St John Prodromos near Serres. Anna Marava-Chatzinikolaou and Christina Touphexi-Paschou, Κατάλογος Μικρογραφικῶν βυζαντινῶν χειρογράφων τῆς Ἐθνικῆς Βιβλιοθήκης τῆς Ἑλλάδος, II (Athens, 1985), no. 12, pp. 60–75, plates 121–39. See now: R. S. Nelson and J. Lowden, 'The Palanologina Group. Additional manuscripts and new questions', *DOP*, XLV (1991), 59–68.

[35] R. Devreesse, *Bibliothèque Nationale. Catalogue des manuscrits grecs*, II: *Le fond Coislin* (Paris, 1945), p. 122. The Commentaries of Theophylact are in *MPG*, vol. 123.

punishment traditionally inflicted on unsuccessful pretenders to the throne was to be deprived of their sight. It is sad to report that Theodora's peace mission failed. The revolt of Philanthropenos was crushed in December 1295 and he was blinded.[36]

Theodora went back to her devotions and her scholarship in her convent in Constantinople and nothing further is known about her career. She died five years later, on 6 December 1300. The notice of her death is inscribed on a manuscript of Thucydides which once belonged to her friend and protégé Maximos Planoudes. She probably gave it to him before she died and he alone recorded on it the hour, the day, the month and the year of her passing.[37] For him, as for so many of the literati of her day, she was 'my revered lady, the well-born nun Theodora Raoulaina Kantakouzene Komnene Palaiologina, cousin of the most pious Emperor Andronikos'. She would have enjoyed the recital of her aristocratic lineage. She would have been proud that her obituary was written by so famous a scholar.

[36] Pachymeres, *De Andronico Palaeologo*, II, pp. 208–20, 220–32 (*CSHB*). D. M. Nicol, *The Last Centuries of Byzantium, 1261–1453*, 2nd ed. (Cambridge, 1993), pp. 130–2.

[37] M. Théarvić, 'Notes de chronologie byzantines', *EO*, IX (1906), 298–300; Kugéas, 'Zur Geschichte', 590–1. The note is wrongly transcribed by Lambros, *NE*, XVIII (1924), 275.

━━━━ ❰❱ ━━━━

CHAPTER FOUR

EIRENE PALAIOLOGINA
(YOLANDA OF MONTFERRAT),
EMPRESS, 1288/9–1317

YOLANDA, as she was known to her parents in Italy, became a Byzantine by marriage; and her marriage, like those of the Greek princesses Helena and Thamar, was a diplomatic and political arrangement calculated to suit the purposes of her father and her husband. The Montferrat family of Lombardy into which she was born had had connexions with Byzantium since the time of the Fourth Crusade. Boniface Marquis of Montferrat, the leader of that expedition, had been allotted what he liked to call the 'Kingdom' of Thessalonica as his part of the spoils of the Latin conquest of Constantinople and the Byzantine Empire in 1204. It was a short-lived kingdom. The title to it, however, remained with the Montferrat family. It had indeed, or so they claimed, been granted to their ancestors before the Fourth Crusade about 1180, when the Emperor Manuel I conferred it upon the brother of Boniface, Rainier of Montferrat, who married the Emperor's daughter.[1]

Yolanda's father was the Marquis William VII. Her mother was Beatrice of Castile. She married Andronikos II Palaiologos, who had come to the throne in Constantinople in December 1282. His father Michael VIII had lost the loyalty of his people by engineering the union between the eastern and western churches. Almost the first act of his son was to declare that union to be null and void. It may seem strange that he should at once have looked for a wife who was a westerner by birth and faith. Politics rather than religion dictated his choice. His first wife had been Anne of Hungary, who died in 1281 leaving him two sons, Michael and Constantine. Marriage to a Byzantine Emperor was still

---

[1] There are two monographs on Eirene: C. Diehl, *Figures Byzantines*, series II (Paris, 1908), p. 226–45 (also in Diehl, *Impératrices de Byzance* (Paris, 1959)); Hélène Constantinidi-Bibikou, 'Yolande de Montferrat impératrice de Byzance', *L'Hellénisme Contemporain*, 2nd ser., IV (1950), 425–42. See also S. Runciman, 'Thessalonica and the Montferrat inheritance', *Gregorios o Palamas*, XLII (1959), 27–34; *PLP*, IX, no. 21361.

thought to be a good catch among the ruling classes in the west. The Popes naturally disapproved of it, especially if the male partners were so openly committed as Andronikos to rejecting the claims of the church of Rome. The diplomats of the Byzantine court were well enough briefed to know their way through the labyrinth of western politics and religion in the struggle between Angevins and Aragonese. The western monarch to whom Andronikos directed them was Alfonso X of Castile. He had no daughter of his own to send to Constantinople. But he was happy to send his grand-daughter, Yolanda of Montferrat. She was escorted to Constantinople by three Genoese ships and her marriage was celebrated in 1284 according to the Orthodox rite. She was about eleven years old and her husband the Emperor twenty-five or twenty-six.[2]

Yolanda was thereafter known by the Greek name of Eirene. Her father as Marquis of Montferrat had inherited the title to the 'Kingdom' of Thessalonica but confessed that he derived no practical benefit from it. The Emperor Andronikos II found it politically convenient to recognise that the house of Montferrat had hereditary rights of some kind over the second city of his Empire. His marriage to Yolanda-Eirene solved the nagging problem of those rights. For as her dowry she surrendered them to him. In return the Emperor paid to her father a substantial sum of money and undertook to maintain a company of 500 horsemen in Lombardy every year. It was an expensive contract and the dividends which the Emperor gained were not those which he had expected. When she was a child-bride Yolanda-Eirene was said to be charming, well-mannered and pretty.[3] In later life she became vain, sour, jealous and troublesome; and she came to regard her dowry of Thessalonica as her own property. Her husband who at first adored her found her increasingly difficult to understand. No doubt she became outwardly byzantinised. She had no urge to return to the land of her birth. But mentally and culturally she remained a westerner with a different view of the way the world was run.

In the early years of her marriage she bore him three sons, John, Theodore and Demetrios, and one daughter Simonis. He crowned her as his Empress after the birth of her first son in 1286.[4] It was taken for granted in Byzantine society that the Emperor's two sons by his first marriage should take precedence over Eirene's children. She could

---

[2] George Pachymeres, *De Andronico Palaeologo*, II, p. 87 (*CSHB*); Nikephoros Gregoras, *History. Byzantina Historia*, ed. L. Schopen, I, p. 168 (*CSHB*), who specifically notes that the marriage was arranged without the approval or consent of the Pope. Angeliki E. Laiou, *Constantinople and the Latins. The foreign policy of Andronicus II, 1282–1328* (Cambridge, Mass., 1972), pp. 45–8 (cited hereafter as Laiou, *Andronicus II*).

[3] Gregoras, I, p. 168. [4] Pachymeres, *De Andronico Palaeologo*, II, pp. 87–8.

probably understand this but, as the years went on, she resented it. Before he married her the Emperor had signified that his heir and successor to the throne was his first-born son Michael; and he confirmed the fact by getting the Patriarch to crown him as co-Emperor (Michael IX) in May 1294. In the same year he conferred on his second son Constantine the imperial title of Despot.[5] Eirene began to feel that the sons she had borne him were being left out of account. They were still young. The eldest, John Palaiologos, had been born in 1286 and so was no more than eight years old when his half-brother Michael was crowned as co-Emperor. Eirene, however, made such a fuss that her husband had to pacify her by granting the boy the title of Despot.[6] Eirene was still not satisfied. The historian Nikephoros Gregoras paints a very unflattering picture of her. He disliked westerners in general. But of Eirene he particularises that she was arrogant and ambitious by nature. She was ambitious for herself but also for the well-being and prospects of her children; for she looked upon her three boys and one girl as her own. She wanted to ensure that her sons and their children and their children's children would perpetuate the memory of their mother by reigning over the Empire of the Romans. This, she thought, could be achieved by dividing that Empire into principalities, one for each to rule as an independent Emperor, though subject in theory to the first-born Emperor Michael.

What Eirene proposed was nothing less than the partition of the single Empire or monarchy of the Romans, an institution hallowed by the antiquity of Roman law, into a number of hereditary appanages, one for each of her sons as if they were private property. Her husband was horrified. He told her that her proposal was out of the question. It was unthinkable and impossible thus to make a polyarchy out of the monarchy of the Romans which had been ordained by God so many centuries before. He would never permit it.[7]

Gregoras, reporting on Eirene's suggestion, accuses her of wishing to introduce western forms of government into the Roman Empire. 'For she was a Latin by birth and it was from the Latins that she picked up this novel idea.' The novel idea has been construed as a form of feudalism and no doubt it was, even though Eirene can hardly have been conscious of the fact. She had left Italy when she was only eleven

[5] Ibid., p. 195; Gregoras, I, p. 193. *PLP*, IX, nos. 21499 (Constantine), 21529 (Michael IX). Laiou, *Andronicus II*, p. 32 note 1.

[6] Pachymeres, *De Andronico Palaeologo*, II, p. 197. *PLP*, IX, no. 21475 (John).

[7] Gregoras, I, pp. 233–5; Pseudo-Phrantzes, *Chronicon maius*, ed. V. Grecu, p. 172. Laiou, *Andronicus II*, p. 229; J. W. Barker, 'The problem of Byzantine appanages during the Palaiologan period', *Byzantina*, III (1971), 103–22.

years old, since when she had been living in Constantinople, probably
in the seclusion of the women's quarters in the imperial palace. It is hard
to believe that she had been spending her time studying feudal law and
political theory in the rare intervals between bearing her husband's children. Gregoras was not attracted to the Latins and their way of life, but
as a scholar he may well have known that Eirene's idea of dividing the
Empire into separate and hereditary principalities smacked of western
European theory and practice. At the end of the thirteenth century it
was still, as he says, a 'novelty' to the Byzantines as true Romans and
foreign to their tradition. Fifty years later their own Emperors were to
introduce something akin to this novelty by apportioning what was left
of the provinces of their Empire as appanages to the sons of their own
family, though not as their hereditary property. Unless the concept of
feudalism was inbred in Eirene at a tender age it is hard to suppose that
she would have understood it as such. It must rather have seemed to her
a perfectly simple and practicable way of satisfying her maternal instinct
to safeguard the present and future careers of her children. She may also
have suggested it out of vindictiveness against her husband. For she had
come to dislike him. Andronikos II was a most pious Emperor devoted
to theology and philosophy, a patron of scholarship and the arts. But he
was a demanding man as a husband and he must have been difficult to
live with. His sexual prowess was abundant and he had at least two
illegitimate children. Eirene accused him of being an old goat when she
was cross with him.[8]

She was certainly cross over his stubborn refusal to grant her wishes
with regard to her sons. She tried all manner of feminine wiles upon
him, now bursting into hysterical tears, now threatening suicide, now
tempting him with her coquetry and then refusing him her bed, until
the Emperor could bear her tantrums no longer. His love for her faded.
He was concerned and frightened that their noisy disagreement might
become public knowledge and cause scandal.[9] Their relationship was
further strained when the Emperor insisted that, for reasons of state,
their daughter Simonis must be sacrificed as a bride to appease the Kral
of Serbia, Stephen Milutin (1281–1321), whose activities were threatening the frontiers of Macedonia and the city of Thessalonica. He had
asked for the hand of a Byzantine princess as his price for keeping the
peace. The Emperor thought that his own sister Eudokia might serve;
but Eudokia rudely refused to be a pawn in her brother's diplomacy.
His daughter by Eirene was the only available alternative. Simonis

[8] Laiou, *Andronicus II*, p. 8.   [9] Gregoras, I, p. 235.

could not complain for she was only five years old. Others, however, complained and protested on her behalf, notably the Patriarch of Constantinople who objected strongly on the grounds of Milutin's age and debauchery. For the Serbian king was in his fifties and had a chequered moral career of previous marriages and bigamy. Eirene's reactions are not recorded. She must, however, have thought that here was another example of her husband's contempt for the children that she had borne him; and later she was to discover that having a foot in the court of Serbia gave her another weapon with which to torment him. The scandalous marriage of the child Simonis to the middle-aged lecher Milutin took place at Thessalonica in April 1299. It was probably the last occasion when Eirene and her husband appeared together in public.[10]

She had lost her little daughter in more ways than one. For King Milutin proved unable to contain himself for the consummation of their marriage and rendered the poor girl incapable of ever bearing children. Eirene was determined that she alone would arrange the marriages and the careers of her sons, John, Theodore and Demetrios. For John, the eldest, she envisaged a wedding to Isabelle of Villehardouin, widow of the French Prince of Achaia in the Peloponnese. Again the Emperor intervened and decreed that John should marry Eirene Choumnaina, daughter of his favourite minister of state, Nikephoros Choumnos, and sent him off with his bride to govern Thessalonica.[11] It was a great honour for the family of Choumnos but a bitter disappointment for John's mother. She decided that she could stand no more of her husband's interference. About Easter 1303 she packed her bags and left Constantinople and the palace to take up residence in Thessalonica.[12] It was after all part of her dowry as the Montferrat inheritance in Byzantium. There she would be nearer to her daughter Simonis and to her son John; and there she stayed for most of the rest of her life, holding court as Empress in her own right. In January 1305 her own brother, the Marquis of Montferrat in Lombardy, died. The title passed to her and she planned to confer it on her son John. She almost persuaded her husband that John would have a greater future as Marquis of Montferrat than as governor of Thessalonica. But the Patriarch of Constantinople, Athanasios, was shocked when he heard of the plan. Athanasios was something of a saint and something of a puritanical reformer. He was also an incorrigible anti-Latin bigot. The Emperor was mesmerised by him and quickly changed his mind about the future

[10] Pachymeres, De Andronico Palaeologo, ii, pp. 275–7; Gregoras, i, pp. 203–4. Laiou, Andronicus II, pp. 95–100.

[11] On Eirene Choumnaina, see below, pp. 59–69.   [12] Gregoras, i, pp. 235, 241–4.

of his son John. The Patriarch took the trouble to write him a letter warning him that it would do John's immortal soul no good to send him to live among arrogant and senseless barbarians in a foreign land. He also advised that it would be better if John did not see his mother for a while. The young man died two years later in Thessalonica with his immortal soul unsullied by life in Italy.[13]

Eirene had been thwarted yet again. She may have felt that the purity of the Orthodox faith which the Patriarch Athanasios cherished above all else was a mixed blessing. She applied her mind to the future of her second son Theodore. She had thought that he might marry a daughter of Guy II de la Roche, the French Duke of Athens. The Duke was not interested. She therefore proposed that Theodore should inherit the title to the Marquisate of Montferrat in place of John. He left for the 'foreign land' of Italy in 1306 and married a lady of the family of Spinola from Genoa. He was rarely seen in Byzantine circles again except to beg money from his parents to pay his debts, and he condemned himself in the Patriarch's eyes by adopting the Roman faith. He died in Lombardy in 1338.[14] Eirene regarded Thessalonica as her own property and her own domain. There as Empress she controlled her own finances and conducted her own foreign policy without reference to her husband in Constantinople. She had her own country estate in Drama in eastern Macedonia to which she retreated from time to time. To begin with, for almost two years from 1303 to 1305, her husband insisted that she should have the services of Theodore Metochites as her counsellor and administrator but also as a spy to keep an eye on her subversive activities. For he did not trust her.[15]

His suspicions were justified. In Thessalonica she mounted a campaign of vicious innuendo and open vilification of him. The accusations which she shamelessly circulated against her husband's morals and character would be almost unbelievable were they not recorded, with some relish, by the later Byzantine historian Nikephoros Gregoras, himself a pupil of Theodore Metochites. 'Hell', as he remarks in rather similar language, 'hath no fury like a woman scorned.' Eirene's stories about

13 Athanasios I, *Letters. The Correspondence of Athanasios I Patriarch of Constantinople*, ed. Alice-Mary Maffry Talbot (*CFHB*, vii: Washington, D.C., 1975), no. 84, pp. 220–7, 410–14. Gregoras, i, p. 241. Laiou, *Andronicus II*, p. 173.

14 Angeliki E. Laiou, 'A Byzantine prince latinized: Theodore Palaeologus, Marquis of Montferrat', *B*, xxxviii (1968), 386–410; F. Cognasso, 'Una crisobolla di Michaele IX Paleologo per Teodoro I di Monferrato', *Studi Bizantini*, ii (1927), 39–47.

15 See I. Ševčenko, *La vie intellectuelle et politique à Byzance sous les premiers Paléologues. Etudes sur la polémique entre Théodore Métochites et Nicéphore Choumnos* (Brussels, 1962), Appendix iii, pp. 275–9.

life with the Emperor, bruited about in private and in public without fear of God or man, were such as to bring a blush to the cheeks of the most shameless courtesans. Even monks and noble ladies who frequented her court were treated to her scandalous and wicked gossip about her husband's private life.[16] The most sinister and destructive of her ploys was her relationship with her son-in-law in Serbia. She had settled in Thessalonica partly to get away from her husband and partly to be nearer to her daughter Simonis, who had been forced to marry the Serbian Kral, Stephen Milutin. Eirene saw in Milutin another agent of her vendetta against her husband. She forgave him his ill-treatment of her daughter. She corresponded with him, showered him with money and gifts and invited him to her court. She even fitted him out with a crown to wear which she replaced every year with a more lavishly bejewelled version. She knew well enough that she was fostering a long-standing Serbian ambition to take over Macedonia and the city of Thessalonica. She was playing a dangerous diplomatic game calculated to embarrass her husband the Emperor. When it was clear that Milutin was never going to produce a son by his child wife whose future he had wrecked, Eirene persuaded him to adopt as his heir her last unmarried son Demetrios, who was with her in Thessalonica. She sent him to Serbia laden with presents and money. But Demetrios found the barbarity and tedium of the Serbian court more than he could bear; and after not much more than a year he came back.[17] Later she made her other son, the Marquis Theodore, when he was on one of his rare visits to her, spend some time at the Serbian court. But he too found it unbearable and hurried back to his wife in Lombardy. Gregoras goes so far as to say that Eirene hoped that the Serbians would in the end take over Thessalonica and the whole of the Byzantine Empire, for it would be of benefit to her children.[18]

Stephen Milutin of Serbia was Eirene's closest and most powerful ally in her feud with her husband Andronikos. But there may have been others. In 1303, when the Turks were ravaging his eastern frontiers, he had unwisely enlisted the services of a band of professional mercenaries from the west known as the Catalan Company. They were an unruly lot and did more harm than good in their sporadic fighting in Asia Minor. They rebelled and set themselves up in Thrace from where they had to be forcibly ejected. Their most lasting achievement was their conquest from the French of the Duchy of Athens and Thebes in 1311.

---

[16] Pachymeres, *De Andronico Palaeologo*, II, pp. 378–9; Gregoras, I, pp. 235–7.

[17] Gregoras, I, pp. 241–4.

[18] On Demetrios Palaiologos, see *PLP*, IX, no. 21546.

Plate 1   Theodora Komnene Palaiologina (nun Theodoule) with her
daughter (Lincoln College, Oxford; *typikon* f. 11ʳ)

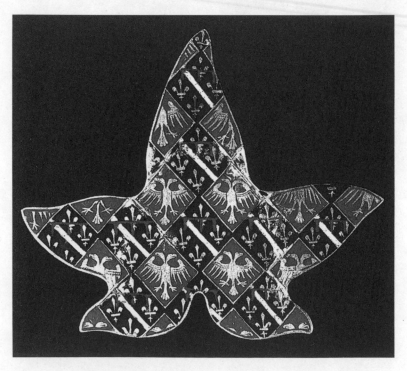

Plate 2   Gold enamelled locket presented by Thamar of Epiros to her husband Philip of Taranto, 1294 (Museo Archeologico Nazionale, Cividale del Friuli)

Plate 3 Simonis, bride of Stephen Milutin of Serbia (wall painting
from Gračanica)

Plate 4   Empress Anna of Savoy (Würtembergische Landesbibliothek, Stuttgart; Cod. Hist. 2-601, f. 4)

Plate 5 Manuscript written by Theodora Raoulaina
(Biblioteca Apostolica Vaticana; Cod. Vat. gr. 1899)

Plate 6   Bookplate of the *Etymologikon* of 1499, printed in Venice at
the expense of Anna Notaras (Gennadius Library, Athens)

Plate 7   The meeting of the two princesses (Biblioteca Apostolica
Vaticana; Cod. Vat. gr. 1851)

Plate 8   Mara Branković (detail from chrysobull of 1420 in
Esphigmenou monastery, Mt Athos)

But there had been those in the west who looked on the Catalans as the advance guard of a crusade for the restoration of the long-lost Latin Empire of Constantinople. The venture could be dressed up in the guise of a crusade against the Turks for the rescue of Constantinople. The leading champion of the venture was Charles of Valois, brother of Philip IV of France, for he had married Catherine of Courtenay, heiress to the title of the Latin Emperors of Constantinople. He was in alliance with Frederick II of Aragon and with Serbia. His hopes were flattered by a few officials in the Byzantine world, looking not so much for a foreign Emperor as for help against the Turks. Letters survive which some of them wrote to Charles of Valois. One of them was John Monomachos, acting governor of Thessalonica at the time. There is little direct evidence that Eirene was involved in their plans. But it would suit her purposes well if a Latin Empire of Constantinople could be revived; and it could be profitable for her children.[19]

The enterprise remained a fantasy and was soon shelved if not forgotten. Eirene's rage against her husband seems to have abated as her projects for the advancement of her own family fell through. Her son Theodore had found his inheritance in Montferrat. Her son Demetrios had declined to be made heir to the Serbian throne and before long left Thessalonica for Constantinople, where he indulged in the quieter pursuits of writing and painting. John the Despot had died in Thessalonica in 1307 and his widow, whom Eirene had never liked, went off to take up a new life as a nun.[20] It may have been after John's death that Eirene, feeling deserted and disappointed, thought of going back to Constantinople herself to try to patch things up with her husband and resume her place in palace life. It appears that she was not well briefed about the hazards of the neighbourhood, for she had not got far on her journey when a message reached her to say that she was in danger of being apprehended by the Catalans who were in command of the route. She hurried back to Thessalonica, which was saved from Catalan attacks by the timely intervention of an army from Constantinople.[21]

She certainly visited her husband at a later stage but reconciliation was probably impossible. She had gone too far in her denunciation of him. The Patriarch Athanasios grieved in his heart about the rift between the Emperor and his wife. He wrote to Eirene implying that her broken marriage was a bad example to the less fortunate orders of

---

[19] Constantinidi-Bibikou, 'Yolande de Montferrat', 435–9; Laiou, *Andronicus II*, pp. 213, 219.
[20] See below, pp. 59–69.
[21] Pachymeres, *De Andronico Palaeologo*, II, pp. 586–7; Gregoras, I, p. 245.

society. Since his letter is addressed to her after her arrival in the capital, it confirms that she made at least one attempt to see her husband. The Patriarch refers to the 'lengthy separation' between them and prays that it may come to an end and that love will triumph over bitterness. He complains that he had not known the full seriousness of the matter. The Emperor had tried to keep it quiet, which was perhaps easier to do in Constantinople than in Thessalonica where Eirene's lurid tales about his conduct must have been common knowledge.[22] In another letter to the Emperor, however, the Patriarch hints at 'the whispered reproaches of certain persons against him' and recommends continence and the peace that comes with it. It is of course possible that he is here referring to the mistress whom Andronikos had taken by way of consolation. Finally, since reconciliation between Andronikos and Eirene seemed no nearer, the Patriarch suggested that he and the Emperor should have a private talk either in the palace or in one of the city churches as soon as possible, to bring peace and harmony with the wife whom God had granted him. He knew that it would be difficult, for she was strong-willed and possessed of the arrogance common among people of her race.[23] He spoke the truth about Eirene's strong will and arrogance, though they were vices not confined to westerners. There is no evidence that his counsel and concern had any effect on Eirene's marriage. The Patriarch's correspondence ends at the end of his second term of office, in September 1309; and the contemporary historians have no more to say about Eirene, except that she died in her private Empire of Thessalonica in 1317, at her country seat at Drama where she had been taken ill of a fever. Simonis came from Serbia for her mother's funeral and later accomplished the removal of her mortal remains to Constantinople to be laid in the monastery of the Pantokrator.[24]

In her will she distributed most of her great wealth among her children. The residue was to be spent on necessary repairs to the church of St Sophia in Constantinople. Monodies or funeral orations on her were written by Alexios Lampenos of Thessalonica and by Theodore Hyrtakenos, the scholar of Constantinople. Poems about her life and death were composed by the court poet Manuel Philes and by Theodore Metochites, who had known her in Thessalonica.[25] Hyrtakenos

[22] Talbot, *Correspondence of Athanasios I*, no. 75, pp. 187–91, 397–8.
[23] *Ibid.*, nos. 97, 98, pp. 252–5, 427–8.
[24] Gregoras, I, p. 273.
[25] Alexios Lampenos, *Monodies*, ed. Sp. P. Lambros, *NE*, XI (1914), 359–400 (377–82). Hyrtakenos, ed. J. F. Boissonade, *Anecdota Graeca*, I (Paris, 1829), pp. 269–81. Manuel Philes, ed. Ae. Martini, *Manuelis Philae Carmina Inedita* (Naples, 1900), no. 7, pp. 13–17. Metochites: see I. Ševčenko, 'Theodore Metochites, the Chora, and the

described her as 'the flower of all the virtues and the noblest of the fruits of the nobility'. Philes is more factual, at least about her antecedents and her offspring. He alone records the names of her three other children: Isaac, Bartholomew and Theodora, who seem to have died in infancy. Both writers are tactfully reticent about her stormy private life. Yet for all her shortcomings and faults of character, her religious beliefs were correct. She never reverted to her ancestral Roman faith and her name was enrolled and remembered in the list of pious Orthodox Empresses.[26] That she governed her appanage in Thessalonica as Empress in her own right is witnessed by a number of documents issued by her as Augusta or Despoina. Much of her property in Macedonia had been made over to her freehold by her husband, either to win her affection or to appease her ill-feeling towards him.[27] She employed her own administrator and accountants to run her estates, which included the district of Serres and her country retreat at Drama.[28] Several of the lead seals survive which she impressed on her official documents. They show her crowned and labelled as Eirene the most pious Augusta Komnene Doukaina Palaiologina. She was evidently proud to belong to her husband's imperial family, if not to the man himself.[29]

Her daughter Simonis was the last unhappy sacrificial victim of Eirene's diplomacy. Having attended her mother's burial in Constantinople she had no desire to return to the arms of her barbarous husband in Serbia. She felt free. She confessed that she was afraid of him. After about a year he sent messengers to fetch her and threatened war if she was not at once returned to him. Her father the Emperor told her that she must go and delivered her to the Serbians who had come for her. Along the way, however, she slipped her lead and dressed herself up in a nun's habit. As such she was unassailable. Her escorts were at a loss. They could neither coerce her nor go on without her. They feared the worst if they returned to Serbia empty-handed. It was her half-brother

intellectual trends of his time', in P. Underwood, ed., *The Kariye Djami*, IV (Princeton, N.J., 1975), pp. 19–91 (especially p. 28).

[26] J. Gouillard, 'Le Synodikon de l'Orthodoxie. Edition et commentaire', *TM*, II (1967), 101.

[27] Chrysobull of Andronikos II to Eirene: *MM*, V (Vienna, 1887), pp. 268–70; *DR*, V, no. 2158 (where the document is dated to just before the coronation of Michael IX in May 1294). Constantinidi-Bibikou, 'Yolande de Montferrat', 434–5.

[28] P. Lemerle, *Philippes et la Macédoine orientale* (Paris, 1945), pp. 187–9. P. Lemerle, ed., *Actes de Kutlumus (Archives de l'Athos)*, II² (Paris, 1988)), nos. 8, 11, pp. 50–53, 60–64. F. Barišić, 'Povelje vizantijskich carica', *ZRVI*, XIII (1971), 159–65.

[29] G. Zacos and A. Veglery, *Byzantine Lead Seals*, I, part 1 (Basel, 1972), no. 125, pp. 120–1; J. Touratzoglou, 'Les sceaux byzantins en plomb de la collection Michael Ritzos au Musée de Thessaloniki', *Byzantina*, V (1973), 272–3.

Constantine, then governor of Thessalonica, who solved the problem by violently stripping her of her disguise as a nun and handing her over to continue her journey to the Serbian court. She was dragged there in floods of tears. She had to endure three more years of terror and misery before her fearsome old husband Stephen Milutin died in October 1321. She hurried back to Constantinople to give thanks for her release by entering a convent, where she died some twenty years later as a fully professed and not fictitious nun, unassailable at last.[30]

[30] Gregoras, I, pp. 287-8, 318. Laiou, *Andronicus II*, pp. 282-3. On Simonis Palaiologina, see M. Laskaris, *Vizantiske prinzese u srednevekovnoj Srbiji* (Belgrade, 1926), pp. 53-82; H. Hunger and O. Kresten, 'Archaisierende Minuskel und Hodegonstil im 14. Jahrhundert. Der Schreiber Theoktistos und die κράλαινα τῶν Τριβαλῶν', *JÖB* xxix (1980), 187-236, especially 223-33; *PLP*, ix, no. 21398. Contemporary wall-paintings of her as the *kralaina* of Stephen Milutin are to be seen in the churches of Staro Nagoričino, Studenica and Gračanica in Serbia.

———— ❦❦❧ ————

CHAPTER FIVE

EIRENE-EULOGIA CHOUMNAINA PALAIOLOGINA, PRINCESS AND ABBESS, DIED c. 1355

EIRENE was the second daughter of Nikephoros Choumnos. She was born in 1291. Little is known about her mother, still less about her upbringing and education. There were those in her lifetime who heaped praises upon her for her literacy and learning. The evidence of her own writings, however, does not reveal a very high standard of expertise in the grammar and spelling of the Greek language. As a child she can hardly have failed to breathe in her father's academic aura, for Nikephoros Choumnos was a dedicated and prolific scholar. He was a brilliant and trusted civil servant who rose to the exalted rank of first secretary (*epi tou kanikleiou*) and prime minister of the Emperor Andronikos II Palaiologos in 1295 until he was upstaged by his former friend and later rival Theodore Metochites. For a short period in 1309–10 he acted as governor of Thessalonica where his family were landed proprietors on a big scale. He and his wife were famously rich. In the midst of his busy political career he found time to compose numerous rhetorical, philosophical and theological works, to keep up a wide correspondence and, above all, to help inspire the revival of interest in classical Greek studies which flourished at the court of Andronikos II. As a youth he had been a pupil of George of Cyprus, the later Patriarch Gregory II (1283–9); and it was doubtless from his master that Nikephoros learnt the joys of expressing his thoughts in simulated Attic Greek and of trying to accommodate as much as possible of ancient Greek philosophy to the Holy Scriptures of the Christian revelation.[1]

[1] J. Verpeaux, *Nicéphore Choumnos homme d'état et humaniste byzantin (ca 1250/1255–1327)* (Paris, 1959); J. Verpeaux, 'Notes prosopographiques sur la famille Choumnos', *BS*, xx (1959), 253–66. Studies of Eirene, the nun Eulogia, include the following: V. Laurent, 'Une princesse byzantine au cloître. Irène-Eulogie Choumnos Paléologue, fondatrice du couvent de femmes τοῦ Φιλανθρώπου Σωτῆρος', *EO*, xxix (1930), 29–60; V. Laurent, 'La direction spirituelle à Byzance. La correspondance d'Irène-Eulogie Choumnaina Paléologue avec son second directeur', *REB*, xiv (1956), 48–86;

His daughter Eirene evidently inherited some of her father's love of scholarship. But she inherited rather more of her mother's piety and devotion to the Christian religion. It was in any case rare for a girl to receive in childhood the formal education that might equip her for a scholarly career; and Eirene was hardly allowed the time for it. Her parents had other ideas in mind for her future. They had been content, for they were both pious Christians, to place her elder sister as a novice in a convent at an early age. There she passed the whole of her life in the blameless obscurity of the cloister. For Eirene they had more materialistic ambitions. They lacked neither money nor influence and Nikephoros was one of the closest confidants of the Emperor Andronikos II. He was also a social climber, as the puritanical Patriarch Athanasios rudely observed.[2] It was the Emperor who proposed that the young Eirene should marry the Emperor of Trebizond, Alexios II, who had ascended the throne of his miniature Empire in 1297. His proposal had to be dropped, however, when Alexios abruptly announced that he was marrying a princess from Georgia.[3] Eirene was hardly out of her infancy. But to her father's delight, it was then suggested that she should become the wife of the Emperor's son John Palaiologos, who had already been given the title of Despot and the expectation of succeeding to his father's throne in due course. Eirene's parents, having lost the chance of gaining a provincial Emperor as their son-in-law, were quick to seize the even more glorious opportunity of elevating their daughter to the position of a potential Empress of Constantinople. The Emperor's wife, Yolanda of Montferrat, disapproved of the scheme. The Despot John was her son and she had hoped that he would marry someone more exalted than the daughter of a mere civil servant, however brilliant.

Yolanda disapproved of most of her husband's schemes, however, and the wedding took place soon after Easter 1303. Eirene had barely reached the canonical age for marriage of twelve years old. Her husband the Despot John Palaiologos was seventeen. As the wife of a Despot she was entitled to call herself *basilissa*, a title of which she was very proud

Angela C. Hero, 'Irene-Eulogia Choumnaina Palaiologina Abbess of the Convent of Philanthropos Soter in Constantinople', *BF*, IX (1985), 119–47; A. C. Hero, *A Woman's Quest for Spiritual Guidance: The correspondence of Princess Irene Eulogia Choumnaina Palaiologina* (Brookline, Mass., 1986); A. C. Hero, 'The unpublished letters of Theoleptos Metropolitan of Philadelphia (1283–1322)', *Journal of Modern Hellenism*, III (1986), 1–31; IV (1987), 1–17. See also, I. Ševčenko, *La vie intellectuelle et politique sous les premiers Paléologues. Etudes sur la polémique entre Théodore Métochites et Nicéphore Choumnos* (Brussels, 1962), pp. 118–25.

[2] Verpeaux, *Nicéphore Choumnos*, pp. 44–52.

[3] George Pachymeres, *De Andronico Palaeologo*, II, pp. 287–9 (*CSHB*). Laurent, 'Une princesse byzantine', 39–40.

and which she retained for the rest of her life, even when she was supposed to have put the pomps of this world behind her. It was a happy marriage, 'truly made in heaven' as a contemporary writer remarked. But it was cut short after less than four years. For early in 1307 the Despot John died in Thessalonica.[4]

Eirene was only sixteen. She was shattered. Her learned father wrote her a stern and studied letter of consolation. It was intended as much to exhibit his own rhetoric as to comfort his desolated and bewildered daughter. For he did not understand her, and he saw her raw and inconsolable grief as a sign of weakness. He was proud to address her as his *basilissa* and to assure her that the whole city from the palace household downwards shared her sorrow. He reminded her that she had brought great honour upon her family; she should not now let them down by over-playing her tragic role. She should, in modern terms, pull herself together. For she had withdrawn into a morbid isolation from society and even from her parents, before whom she refused to appear in her widow's weeds. What she could not find was patience, the patience to endure and overcome the melancholy fate that had been thrust upon her. She must bear in mind that it was her duty to honour and obey her parents instead of retreating into herself and accepting none of their advice and comfort.[5]

She could not marry again without losing rank and so dishonouring the imperial family, a prospect abhorrent to her father. She seemed condemned, young as she was, to spend her days as a dutiful widowed daughter, the showpiece of her parents, living up to her acquired title of *basilissa*. We are not told how long her solitude and sadness lasted. But in the end, much to her father's chagrin, she made up her mind to follow the path of her sister by becoming a bride of Christ. The man who most influenced her in this decision was a monk, a friend of her family, called Theoleptos. He was a born spiritual leader who had been appointed as Bishop of Philadelphia in Asia Minor in 1283. He had suffered persecution for his outspoken opposition to the enforced union of the Byzantine church with Rome in the 1270s. He had become something of a hero through his defence of his see of Philadelphia against the encroaching Turks in 1310. The Emperor much admired

---

[4] Pachymeres *De Andronico Palaeologo*, ii, pp. 289, 377–9; Nikephoros Gregoras, *History, Byzantina Historia*, ed. L. Schopen, i, p. 241 (*CSHB*), who implies that Choumnos twisted the Emperor's arm by flattery and intrigue. On John Palaiologos, born in 1286, see *PLP*, ix, no. 21475.

[5] Nikephoros Choumnos, *Letter* of Consolation to his daughter, ed. J. F. Boissonade, *Anecdota Graeca e Codicibus Regiis*, i (Paris, 1829), pp. 293–305; *MPG*, cxl, cols. 1437–49. Verpeaux, *Nicéphore Choumnos*, pp. 102–3.

him; and he was father confessor to many of the great and good in Constantinople. Theoleptos was a passionate mystic in love with the monastic life which he had embraced when he was twenty-five, abandoning his young and tearful wife to long years of childless widowhood. Perhaps his own callousness enabled him to understand the loneliness of the young Eirene who had been so abruptly bereft of the only love of her life. He helped to persuade her that her salvation lay in her giving herself to God and renouncing the world and all the glories which it had promised her through marriage.[6]

It was Theoleptos who guided her tormented spirit into the peace and quiet of the cloister. It was he who tonsured her as a nun, shearing her 'luxurious golden locks' with his own hand, and receiving her vows of poverty, chastity and obedience. As her spiritual father he wrote her a rather forbidding letter about the problems and responsibilities that she would face in her new vocation.[7] From its outset, however, Eirene made it clear that her monastic life was going to be subject to her own interpretation of the rules and in a convent which she had founded at her own expense. She prevailed upon her parents to subscribe; though she had an ample fortune of her own. She disposed of some of her wealth on the relief of the poor and the ransoming of prisoners-of-war. The rest she devoted to the reconstruction and refurbishment of a deserted monastic building not far from the Great Church of St Sophia. She dedicated it to Christ Philanthropos. It was quite normal practice for members of the imperial family or the nobility in Byzantium to endow or rebuild monastic institutions and to be known thereafter as the founder (*ktitor* or *ktitorissa*). There being no established orders of monks or nuns, it was the founder who drew up the rules or charter (*typikon*) of the new foundation. Only a fragment survives of Eirene's *typikon* for her convent of Christ Philanthropos but it makes a clear statement about her own position. She describes herself as the pious *basilissa* Eirene Laskarina Palaiologina known as Eulogia since she took the veil, for such was the name that she chose when she adopted the 'holy and angelic habit' of a nun. She admits her indebtedness to her parents. But otherwise the rules laid down for the conduct of her nunnery are her own, based though they were on precedent. She may have taken the name of Eulogia in memory of her late husband's great-

---

[6] On Theoleptos, see *PLP*, IV, no. 7509. His five letters are edited with translation by Angela C. Hero, 'The unpublished letters', III, (1986), 1–31; IV (1987), 1–17.

[7] S. Salaville, 'Une lettre et un discours inédits de Théolepte de Philadelphie', *REB*, v (1947), 101–15; Hero, 'The unpublished letters', III, 6–31. See also Theodore Hyrtakenos, *Letters*, ed. J. F. Boissonade, *Anecdota Graeca*, I, (Paris, 1829), p. 287.

aunt, the sister of Michael VIII, who had laboured and suffered in defence of her Orthodox faith.[8]

It has been suggested that she opened her convent about 1312. She cannot have been more than twenty-one years old. It is a measure of the respect that she inspired as a wealthy imperial princess with impressive family connexions that at so young an age she could impose her will on a whole community. For she left no doubt that she had charge of the convent as its superior. She emphasised the fact that it was a *koinobion*, a coenobitic community of nuns sharing everything in common, worshipping, praying, eating and living together under her care and supervision. What the fragment of her *typikon* does not reveal, however, is that the monastery of Christ Philanthropos was unusual in being a double monastery of monks and nuns, segregated and housed in separate though adjacent buildings. Such foundations were from time to time condemned or even prohibited by the church. They became acceptable again in the thirteenth and fourteenth centuries. The puritanical Patriarch Athanasios, who was in office in Eulogia's day, disapproved of them. Yet he founded two double monasteries himself, one being on the hill of Xerolophos in Constantinople. One of their benefits was that the founder's family could lead religious lives at close quarters, as Eulogia's parents were to do after they had each taken monastic vows in 1320.[9] Their daughter, the *basilissa* Eulogia as she styled herself, was the foundress and patroness of the joint institution. Theoleptos of Philadelphia remained her spiritual director, though he was often away from Constantinople ministering to his beleaguered flock in Asia Minor. He advised her by letter, a method which she complained was not at all the same as listening to his advice and comfort by word of mouth. Young as she was, Eirene-Eulogia organised her convent with a strict and jealous competence. Even Theoleptos, many years her senior in age and experience, addressed her as its abbess (*kathigoumeni*). She never pretended, however, that her jurisdiction extended also over the monks next door. They too came under the spiritual direction of Theoleptos; and he produced separate sermons and homilies for the

---

[8] Ph. Meyer, 'Bruchstücke zweier τυπικὰ κτητορικά, *BZ*, IV (1895) 45–58 (text: 48–9). R. Janin, 'Les monastères du Christ Philanthrope à Constantinople', *REB*, IV (1946), 135–62; R. Janin, *La géographie ecclésiastique de l'empire byzantin*, I: *Le siège de Constantinople et le patriarcat oecuménique*; III: *Les églises et les monastères*, 2nd ed., (Paris, 1969), pp. 541–2; R. Trone, 'A Constantinopolitan Double Monastery of the fourteenth century: The Philanthropic Saviour', *Byzantine Studies/Etudes Byzantines*, X, (1983), 81–7. On Eirene-Eulogia, sister of Michael VIII, see pp. 33–40.

[9] Trone, 'A Constantinopolitan Double Monastery'.

monks and for the nuns. He was a hard master, especially for the monks, whose lax and decadent ways he was fond of castigating.[10]

The convent soon became fashionable. It was built, as its foundress had specified, in the sumptuous style befitting an imperial institution, not, as she said, because of her love of luxury but because virtue comes more easily in well-appointed surroundings. Before she died it is said that there were more than a hundred nuns in her care.[11] They were of two classes: the mothers and the sisters. The mothers devoted themselves to prayer and the divine offices; the sisters attended to the domestic affairs of the community. The senior nuns were permitted occasional forays beyond the walls to perform works of charity. Theoleptos indeed recommended visits to the sick and to prisoners provided that they were strictly regulated. Eulogia as abbess received lady visitors in her parlour every Saturday and Sunday when aristocratic friends would keep her informed about the latest events in the city while seeking her spiritual advice and blessing. Her father too came to see her at weekends and through him she kept in touch with some of the leading men of the day, such as the scholar and historian Nikephoros Gregoras and Matthew, Bishop of Ephesos from 1329 to 1351, himself a pupil of Theoleptos. For she found it hard to live her life wholly detached from the world and the court.[12]

Theoleptos warned her against these meetings, reminding her that, as a nun, she was supposed to have renounced her family and her friends. Her regime, however, was strict and strictly enforced. She had a hard streak in her and was often intolerant. She demanded total obedience and subservience from her nuns and quickly lost her patience with any who offended. Theoleptos frequently counselled her to control her nervous impetuosity and impatience and sometimes questioned her judgment in condemning too swiftly those who had gone against her will. There were times when she felt overburdened by the stresses of administration. She had a three-year battle with lawyers to protect her dowry from being misappropriated. Only when her father personally reported the injustice to the Emperor was the matter settled. Then she was taken ill and announced to her adviser that she was thinking of leaving the convent and all its duties and responsibilities to retire to the

[10] Laurent, 'Une princesse byzantine', 52–4.
[11] Gregoras, History, xxix. 22: III, pp. 238–9.
[12] Choumnos, Letters, ed. Boissonade, Anecdota Nova (Paris, 1844), no. 163, pp. 181–2. Hero, A Woman's Quest, pp. 147–8.

solitary peace of a hermitage. Theoleptos was horrified and quickly forbade her ever again to entertain so absurd an idea.[13]

She obeyed him, though fate dealt her many more blows. Theoleptos, who had been the mainstay if not the originator of her spiritual life, was the one man who could make her feel obedient, humble and repentant. He died in faraway Philadelphia in 1322. Just before his death, when he was very elderly, he wrote her a moving letter of farewell.[14] In January 1327 her father Nikephoros Choumnos died as the monk Nathaniel in the monastery alongside her to which he had retired; and soon afterwards her mother died in her daughter's arms as a nun in her own convent. Once again she felt lost and helpless. She mourned the loss of two fathers, the one natural, the other spiritual. But it was the passing of Theoleptos, who had often called her his daughter in religion, that moved her more deeply.[15] Then in 1332 the Emperor Andronikos II, whom she had always esteemed as her father-in-law, died. She became prey to the depression and despair that she had suffered when she had become a young widow. She was about forty years old. What she needed and badly missed was the continuing support and friendship of a spiritual father such as the late Theoleptos.

She found one in a younger monk whose retreat was on the outskirts of Constantinople and not miles away in the provinces. She had often complained to Theoleptos about how unsatisfactory it was to have to bare her soul to him by correspondence. She was soon to find that her new adviser preferred it that way. He had been reluctant to accept her invitation in the first place. Perhaps he was rather afraid of her. She must have had a reputation as an aristocratic and domineering abbess. He seems to have come from Thessalonica where Eulogia's family had many vested interests. He never personally knew Theoleptos and his name remains unknown. But the texts of 22 letters have survived, 14 from himself and 8 from Eulogia, all written in the twelve months of

---

[13] She was so well endowed that her father thought it unnecessary to make further provision for her in his Will, though referring to her as his 'dear *basilissa*'. Choumnos, *Testament*, ed. Boissonade, *Anecdota Graeca*, II, pp. 314–30. Verpeaux, *Nicéphore Choumnos*, pp. 105–6 Laurent, 'Une princesse byzantine', 55–8; Hero, 'Irene-Eulogia', 124–5.

[14] Laurent, 'Une princesse byzantine', 58; Hero, 'The unpublished letters', IV (1987), 1–17. Nikephoros Choumnos, Eulogia's father, at her request, wrote a long Epitaph on Theoleptos, ed. Boissonade, *Anecdota Graeca*, V (Paris, 1823), pp. 183–239. Verpeaux, *Nicéphore Choumnos*, p. 97.

[15] Matthew, Bishop of Ephesos, wrote to console her on Theoleptos's death. L. Previale, 'Due Monodie inedite di Matteo di Efeso', *BZ*, XLI (1941), 4–34 (text: 26–31). Hero, *A Woman's Quest*, letter no. 7; Verpeaux, *Nicéphore Choumnos*, pp. 67–8.

the year 1334–5.[16] They are among the most personal, intimate and confidential documents in all Byzantine literature. Some of their content is more intellectual than spiritual. In her latter years Eulogia appears to have developed an interest in philosophy, in what Byzantine monks were wont to call the 'outer wisdom' of pagan or 'Hellenic' learning, as distinct from the 'inner wisdom' of the spirit. Her father had been a pioneer in the revival of the study of ancient Greek or Hellenic literature fostered by the most pious Christian Emperor Andronikos II. Some monks and church leaders believed that the gap between the inner and the outer wisdom could be judiciously bridged without offending the doctrines of Christianity. Others felt that such intellectual pursuits were a danger to the Christian soul and that they had gone too far. After Andronikos's death a reaction set in which was to culminate in victory for the champions of the unadulterated inner wisdom of the revealed truths of Christianity. In 1334, however, the study of secular, pagan Greek literature and philosophy was still permissible even for monks and nuns. Theoleptos of Philadelphia had not been much in favour of it. Eulogia's new friend and adviser, however, was himself a scholar as well as a monk and he encouraged her in her studies of the heritage of Hellenic literature.

Eulogia had inherited her father's library. Her new adviser described her as the most erudite and cultivated woman of her day, gifted with the wisdom of a man, high praise in Byzantine society.[17] He exaggerated. She herself was conscious of her inability to express her thoughts clearly; and her letters reveal her often imperfect grasp of literary Greek grammar and syntax. None the less she shared her mentor's interest in what could be called humanist studies. Before he became a monk he had written a treatise in defence of Hellenic learning against its detractors and lent it to her in draft form. She was entranced with it and, since he was not a rich man, she promised from time to time to send him paper and money to pay for the copying of others of his works. She would also send him books both sacred and profane from her own collection and a copy of her catalogue of them. It is evident that she was his patroness as well as his pupil.[18]

They had a strange relationship. He was embarrassed by her generosity and her lavish praise of his virtues, intellectual and spiritual. His

[16] Ed. and trans. by Hero, *A Woman's Quest*.
[17] Ed. Hero, *A Woman's Quest*, nos. 2 and 10. Matthew of Ephesos also praised her unique breadth of wisdom and learning. D. Reinsch, ed., *Die Briefe des Matthaios von Ephesos im Codex Vindobonensis Theol. Gr. 174* (Berlin, 1974), no. 32, p. 136. See S. I. Kourousis, Μανουὴλ Γαβαλᾶς, I (Athens, 1972), pp. 188–91, 234–6, 254–6.
[18] Ed. Hero, *A Woman's Quest*, nos. 5, 8, 9, 10, 12. Hero, 'Irene-Eulogia', 130–40.

belief that some Hellenic learning could be relevant to the inner wisdom of Christianity may have reminded her more of her natural father than of her former spiritual director.[19] Their surviving correspondence, however, reveals many more allusions to Scriptural texts than to ancient Greek authors. She disturbed him by repeated invitations to come and visit her, since canon law forbade her from leaving her convent except in dire emergencies, such as the sickness or death of a near relative. Her duty was to stay within her convent walls and serve her nuns, even in the most menial domestic tasks, and to watch over their spiritual development and salvation. Eulogia did what was required of her in such matters; but she still longed for the personal attention of her director. She asked him to visit her regularly six times a year. Somewhat unwillingly he granted her request at least twice, though he annoyed her by insisting that they must meet and talk in the presence of another, elderly monk. He preferred to advise her at arm's length, by correspondence. His letters, extending over a period of no more than twelve months, suggest that, while Eulogia performed her duties as abbess conscientiously and had no doubt grown in spiritual stature, her temperament had not much changed. Theoleptos had often chastised her for being headstrong, arrogant and lacking in patience and tolerance. Her new adviser detected the same faults in her. He reproved her for losing her temper with one of her nuns and hurling javelins of words at her instead of calmly and rationally admonishing her.[20] Nor, it seems, could Eulogia ever forget that she had married into the imperial family. She was not just the foundress, patroness and abbess of a rich and successful convent. She was always and until her death the *basilissa* Palaiologina, a princess in her own right, with a lasting memory of what might have been if her lamented husband had been spared. She complained that, if she ever went out of the convent, her imperial rank dictated that she would have to be accompanied by a retinue of men and horses which she could not afford. Both of her spiritual directors thought that she was too much attached to the ties of family and social standing.

Her correspondence with the second of them in the year 1334–5, was exchanged in the period of political and ecclesiastical calm before the storm. The storm broke in 1341 when the Emperor Andronikos III Palaiologos died. He had reached his throne as a result of civil war. His death provoked a second outbreak of the same malaise. His son and heir John V was only nine years old. His widow, Anna of Savoy, backed by

[19] Ed. Hero, *A Woman's Quest*, nos. 6 and 7; Laurent, 'La direction spirituelle', 60–2.
[20] Ed. Hero, *A Woman's Quest*, nos. 18 and 19.

the Patriarch, opposed the claim of her late husband's closest friend and counsellor, John Cantacuzene, to act as regent. Cantacuzene took to arms and, after six years of fighting, made himself master of Constantinople and Emperor as John VI. The young Emperor John V became his son-in-law. The second civil war caused immense damage to the social and economic structure of what was left of the Empire. It also provoked deep religious dissension. Perhaps only in Byzantium could such a sordid squabble for political and dynastic power have assumed a theological dimension in a dispute over the nature of God and the deification of man. In monastic circles, and particularly on Mount Athos, there was a resurgence of intense spirituality and mysticism in the early fourteenth century. The movement ran parallel to and often at odds with the new renaissance of Hellenic or classical learning fostered by such as Eulogia's father. Its devotees were known as the hesychasts, for their experience of the mysteries of God was to be found in the state of *hesychia* or stillness. The doctrine of the hesychasts was first formulated by the monk Gregory Palamas (1296–1359). The church and society were divided between Palamites and anti-Palamites. Palamas had been greatly influenced by the writings of Eulogia's first mentor, Theoleptos of Philadelphia. The aspiring Emperor John Cantacuzene enjoyed his friendship and support. The Patriarch condemned him and all his works as being heretical. The second civil war was thus partly coloured by the religious persuasions of the opposing factions, Palamites against anti-Palamites, the partisans of Cantacuzene against the loyalists of the family of Palaiologos. In 1351, after the triumph of Cantacuzene and the appointment of a new Patriarch, a council of the church in Constantinople declared the doctrine and practice of the hesychasts to be perfectly in line with Orthodoxy. Palamas, who died in 1359, was canonised as a saint nine years later.[21]

His immense influence as a spiritual leader and a saint put an end to the tentative dabblings of monks and laymen in the new and perilous waters of humanism. For Palamas and his hesychast followers loudly and frequently condemned the study of Hellenic or pagan literature. It was none of a monk's business. Monks should confine their reading to the revealed truths of the Scriptures and the Fathers of the church. In 1334–5, the year of Eulogia's correspondence with her second spiritual director, the storm had not broken. The lines had not been so sharply drawn between humanists and mystics. Her director himself, though

---

[21] J. Meyendorff, *Introduction à l'étude de Grégoire Palamas* (Paris, 1959), pp. 141–53. D. M. Nicol, *The Last Centuries of Byzantium, 1261–1453*, 2nd ed. (Cambridge 1993), pp. 210–14, 232–4.

something of a classical scholar, was a hesychast in theology. What drove the Princess Eulogia into the anti-Palamite camp was her family loyalty to the house of Palaiologos into which she had married. She could not fail to detest John Cantacuzene as an upstart and a usurper. The leading theological opponents of Palamas and the hesychasts found an eloquent and influential ally in Eulogia. Palamas, in not very saintly manner, inveighed against her, belittling her as 'the Choumnaina' not the Palaiologina, a 'small woman invested with some authority', who behaved as if she were a real Empress. The anti-Palamite leaders on the other hand, notably the monk Gregory Akindynos and her friend the historian Nikephoros Gregoras, could not speak too highly of her. She gave shelter to Akindynos when he was on the run. Gregoras described her as 'a true princess' in character and in wisdom. It seems that in championing the twin causes of the dynasty of Palaiologos and true Orthodoxy against the Palamite 'heretics', the *basilissa* Eulogia at last found a fulfilment larger and more satisfying than her tiresome intro-spection and the petty problems of her community with which she had worried her spiritual directors.[22]

She must have rejoiced that the usurper John Cantacuzene was forced to abdicate in December 1354 and that one of her own family of Palaio-logos, John V, came into his inheritance as Emperor. She had been on the winning side in the political battle. In the religious controversy she lost. Cantacuzene had seen to it that his friend Gregory Palamas was elected to the Fathers of Orthodoxy in 1351. Eulogia died a few years later. What she had denounced as the 'heresy' of hesychasm had pre-vailed. Her obstinate persistence in defending her version of the truth of Orthodoxy against the misguided Palamites brought her abuse, derision and even persecution. The struggle took its toll on her failing health. Her last known act, at the end of 1355 when she was gravely ill, was to make over some inherited landed property to a monastery in Mace-donia.[23] She died soon afterwards at the age of about sixty-five. Her friend, the historian and polymath Nikephoros Gregoras applauded to the end her stand against what he too regarded as heresy; and he wrote the nearest thing to a eulogy of her. He described her as a 'true *basilissa*' steeped in knowledge of the Holy Scriptures and theology, a unique exemplar of the monastic life, and the greatest champion of the sacred

[22] Gregoras, *History*, xxix, 21: iii, p. 238. Hero, 'Irene-Eulogia', 140–4; Alice-Mary M. Talbot, 'Blue-stocking nuns. Intellectual life in the convents of late Byzantium', in *Okeanos: Harvard Ukrainian Studies*, vii (*Essays Presented to Ihor Ševčenko*) (Cambridge, Mass., 1984), 604–18.

[23] A. Guillou, *Les archives de Saint-Jean Prodrome sur le mont Ménécée* (Paris, 1955), no. 46, pp. 142–4.

dogmas of the church. Had he lived long enough Gregoras, a practised composer of epitaphs, might have written at greater length in praise of the nun and princess whom he so much admired. He records, however, that the saintly reputation of Eirene-Eulogia among the people of Constantinople was such that pilgrims flocked to her tomb to bask in the odour of her sanctity and to seek her intercession to perform miracles for them.[24] Her scholarship, such as it was, died with her. She left nothing in writing except for the charter of her own convent and her few letters seeking solace, help and guidance in her spiritual progress.

[24] Gregoras, *History*, xxix, 21–4: III, pp. 237–40. Laurent, 'Une princesse byzantine', 58–9.

CHAPTER SIX

─────── ❦ ───────

EIRENE ASENINA CANTACUZENE,
EMPRESS, 1347–1354

AMONG the six children of the Emperor Michael VIII, the founder of the dynasty of Palaiologos, was a daughter called Eirene. In 1279 she was given in marriage to the then Tsar of Bulgaria, John III Asen. She bore him a son called Andronikos Palaiologos Asen who in turn had two sons and two daughters. The elder of his daughters was Eirene Asenina.[1] Nothing is known of her childhood. She was probably brought up in Constantinople, where her brothers John and Manuel Asen rose to high rank at court. About 1318 she married John Cantacuzene, the future Emperor, who was then about twenty-three years old. He was rich and ambitious. He had been brought up as an only child by his widowed mother Theodora whom contemporaries admired for her prudence, judgment and resourcefulness, for her experience in the management of public affairs and her 'more than feminine strength of mind'.[2] Theodora no doubt arranged her son's marriage, having seen in Eirene Asenina a young woman of character and spirit equal to her own. She was not disappointed. At the time of her marriage Eirene's husband held a comparatively humble and purely honorary title, for he and his family were well known at court. To begin with the newly married couple lived at Gallipoli (Kallioupolis) in Thrace, where the Cantacuzene family owned landed estates.[3]

John Cantacuzene was a personal friend and of an age with the young

---

[1] Most of the sources and facts on Eirene's life are collected in: D. M. Nicol, *The Byzantine Family of Kantakouzenos (Cantacuzenus)* (Washington, D.C., 1968), no. 23, pp. 104–08; I. Božilov. *Familijata na Asenevci (1186–1460) Genealogija i Prosopografija* (Sofia, 1985), part 2, no. 17, pp. 307–11; *PLP*, v, no. 10935.

[2] John Cantacuzene, *History*, ed. L. Schopen (*CSHB*, 1828–32), I, p. 125; Nikephoros Gregoras, *History. Byzantina Historia*, ed. L. Schopen (*CSHB* 1829–55), I, p. 530; II, p. 619.

[3] On John (VI) Cantacuzene, see Nicol, *Byzantine Family of Kantakouzenos*, no. 22; *PLP*, v, no. 10973.

Emperor Andronikos III Palaiologos who was disinherited by his disapproving grandfather Andronikos II in 1320. Many of the younger generation of the Byzantine aristocracy felt that he had been wronged and that the time had in any case come for a change of Emperor. John Cantacuzene became the leading light in the rebellion of the jeunesse dorée who championed the cause of Andronikos III against his elderly and incompetent grandfather. He made for Constantinople, leaving Eirene in Gallipoli. She was to become accustomed to being left behind and holding the fort while her husband pursued his ambitions elsewhere. The clique of aristocratic rebels and mere adventurers whom he gathered around him made their headquarters at Adrianople and Didymoteichon in Thrace. There in 1321 the young Andronikos joined them, having escaped the clutches of his grandfather. For over six years desultory civil war was fought, punctuated by unworkable settlements and compromises, until in May 1328 the old Emperor was forced to abdicate and his grandson became sole Emperor in Constantinople as Andronikos III. John Cantacuzene had his reward. He declined to be nominated as co-Emperor. He was content to accept the rank and title of Grand Domestic or commander-in-chief. His wife Eirene and his mother Theodora had both nobly played their part in the struggle, taking joint command of the city of Didymoteichon while the fighting raged elsewhere; and when the fortunes of Andronikos were at a low ebb, Theodora enabled him to pay his troops by financing his operations from her own resources. For Didymoteichon was the centre of the vast wealth of her family.[4]

When Andronikos III died prematurely in 1341 he left an infant son, John Palaiologos. It was widely assumed, not least by Cantacuzene himself, that he would step into the breach as regent of the Empire until the little boy came of age. The boy's mother, Anna of Savoy, was not so sure. She had always mistrusted Cantacuzene's influence over her husband. Her misgivings were shared by the Patriarch of Constantinople and by several less scrupulous opportunists. She and the Patriarch would act as wards of her son and as regents of the Empire. Cantacuzene withdrew with his army to Didymoteichon, prepared to fight for what he and many others believed to be his rights. There in October 1341 his supporters proclaimed him as their Emperor. A second and still more

---

[4] Cantacuzene, I, pp. 28, 52. On the wealth of Cantacuzene and his family in Thrace, see Eva de Vries-Van der Velden, *L'Elite byzantine devant l'avance turque à l'époque de la guerre civile de 1341 à 1354* (Amsterdam, 1989), pp. 82–3. Ursula V. Bosch, *Kaiser Andronikos III. Palaiologos* (Amsterdam, 1965); D. M. Nicol, *The Last Centuries of Byzantium, 1261–1453* (Cambridge, 1993), pp. 167–84.

devastating round of civil war ensued. Again Eirene, now distinguished by the title if not the trappings of an Empress, bravely obeyed her husband's orders. For more than two years she stuck to her post in Didymoteichon while he tried unsuccessfully to win over Thessalonica to his side and was forced to take refuge in Serbia.[5]

By then Eirene had borne him six children. Matthew and Manuel, born about 1325 and 1326, had gone with their father. Her youngest son Andronikos was in Constantinople in the care of his grandmother. Both, however, were held under arrest by the regents; and Theodora was to die sick and impoverished as a result of the treatment that she suffered. Eirene had with her in Didymoteichon her three daughters, Maria, Theodora and Helena. The defence of the city was in the hands of her brother Manuel Asen, for it was constantly subject to raids and attacks from Constantinople. After a while she began to lose hope that her husband would ever get through to join her and she sought help from her neighbours in Bulgaria and from the Turks. Her courageous conduct impressed many at the time. She was embarrassed by the arrival at Didymoteichon of one of her husband's Turkish allies, Umur the Emir of Aydin (Smyrna), who had come uninvited to Gallipoli and marched north hoping to find John Cantacuzene. He camped nearby as an unexpected guest for about three months; and Eirene, thinking that she was doing what her husband would have wanted, supplied his camp with food and clothing in the depth of winter while his soldiers pillaged the coast of Thrace. She must have been glad to be rid of him and his men when, disappointed at not having seen her husband, he led them back to Asia Minor.[6]

It was not until the winter of 1343 that her husband succeeded in fighting his way back to her at Didymoteichon. The wind of his fortunes then began to change and the prospect of his victory in the civil war became clearer. He celebrated his new confidence by allowing himself to be crowned as Emperor, so fulfilling the promise of his proclamation five years before. His coronation was performed at Adrianople on 21 May 1346 by the Patriarch of Jerusalem, who had condemned the regime of his colleague the Patriarch in Constantinople. It was the Byzantine custom that a newly crowned Emperor should invest his wife as Empress with his own hands. John Cantacuzene followed

[5] Nicol, *Last Centuries*, pp. 185–208.
[6] Cantacuzene, II, pp. 336–9, 345–8, 401–5; Gregoras, II, pp. 648–53, 692–3; Doukas, *Istoria Turco-Bizantină*, ed. V. Grecu (Bucharest, 1958), pp. 51–3. P. Lemerle, *L'Emirat d'Aydin, Byzance et l'Occident* (Paris, 1957), p. 150. On the discrepancy in the sources here, see De Vries-Van der Velden, *L'Elite byzantine*, pp. 124–5.

tradition by placing her crown on Eirene's head after his own coronation by the Patriarch. It was her reward for the loyalty that she had shown to his cause during their long separation.[7]

A month later she was required to face an even sterner test of her loyalty and of her maternal instincts. She had to agree that her second daughter Theodora should marry outside the Christian faith. Orhan, the Osmanli Emir of Bithynia in Asia Minor, had been pleased to lend military help to Cantacuzene when he was in difficulties during the war. The two men struck up a strange personal friendship which, in Orhan's opinion, could be strengthened and perpetuated by a marital alliance between the two families. He vowed that he was passionately in love with the young and pretty Theodora Cantacuzene, though it is not clear where he can have seen or met her. It was a distasteful if not sacrilegious union but it suited her father's plans; and in the summer of 1346 Eirene and the rest of her family were obliged to attend the wedding, which took place at Selymbria on the Thracian coast. Cantacuzene in his Memoirs gives a full account of this bizarre ceremony. It was not the first marriage of a Christian princess to a 'barbarian' ruler. Indeed, Cantacuzene justified it by precedent. It must have stretched Eirene's forbearance to the limit. She was no doubt comforted, however, by the news that her daughter Theodora clung tenaciously to her Christian religion after marriage despite many attempts to convert her to Islam. She became a tower of strength to the Christian prisoners and slaves in her husband's realm and a shining example of Christian virtue to all. When Orhan died in 1362, however, she was glad to be allowed to hurry back to Constantinople to the company of her mother and her sisters.[8]

The second civil war at last came to its end at the beginning of February 1347 when John Cantacuzene entered Constantinople and accepted the surrender of the Dowager Empress Anna of Savoy and the Patriarch who had opposed him. It was agreed that he should now reign as senior Emperor with the young John Palaiologos, the son of the late Andronikos III, as his co-Emperor. The partisans of each side in the long and needless conflict were required to swear allegiance to both Emperors; and the peace between the ruling families was to be sealed by the

---

[7] Cantacuzene, II, p. 564. The correct procedure for the coronation of an Empress by her Emperor is described in the fourteenth-century manual of protocol, ed. J. Verpeaux, *Pseudo-Kodinos, Traité des Offices* (Paris, 1966), pp. 260–2.

[8] Cantacuzene, II, pp. 585–9. Nicol, *Byzantine Family of Kantakouzenos*, no. 29, pp. 134–5; A. A. M. Bryer, 'Greek historians on the Turks: the case of the first Byzantine–Ottoman marriage', *The Writing of History in the Middle Ages. Essays presented to R. W. Southern*, ed. R. H. C. Davis and J. M. Wallace-Hadrill (Oxford, 1981), pp. 471–93.

marriage of the junior Emperor John Palaiologos to Cantacuzene's daughter Helena. Eirene was summoned to bring her from Adrianople for the ceremony of her betrothal. On 21 May 1347, the Feast of Saints Constantine and Helena, the new Patriarch of Constantinople performed the second coronation of John Cantacuzene as Emperor. He then for a second time placed an Empress's crown on the head of his wife Eirene. At the end of the month the wedding of their daughter Helena to John Palaiologos was celebrated. He was fifteen years of age and she about a year younger. He needed no second coronation for he had been properly crowned in Constantinople in the first year of the civil war; but he was careful to observe tradition by crowning Helena as his Empress after their wedding.[9]

One wonders how there were so many crowns to meet the demand, for the Empress Anna of Savoy had pawned the original crown jewels to Venice to raise funds during the civil war. Five thrones were produced for the banquet and festivities after the coronation. But the guests sadly noted that the crown jewels were made of glass and the plate for the banquet was not gold and silver but pewter and clay.[10] A note on a manuscript written in August 1351 records that in that year there were five rulers in Byzantium: the Despoina Anna Palaiologina, the Emperor John Palaiologos and his Empress Helena, the Emperor John Cantacuzene and his Empress Eirene. It was not an arrangement calculated to make for stability.[11]

Eirene must have derived more satisfaction and pleasure from Helena's marriage than she did from that of her other daughter Theodora, who had been condemned to live in an alien culture in an infidel land. It is hard to believe that she had much in common with the Dowager Empress Anna of Savoy, who had shown herself to be a weak-minded, bitter and selfish woman in the years of civil war. Her ambition was to protect and foster the rights of her own son, now the junior Emperor John. But Eirene's son Matthew Cantacuzene was far from content with the agreement which his father had made. Matthew was aggrieved at having to play second fiddle to a younger man who had so recently been the sworn enemy of his family. He felt that he and not John Palaiologos should be recognised as heir to his father's throne. Eirene quite possibly felt the same. But she could never go against her husband's wishes. At the first sign of trouble, before the end of 1347, far from encouraging Matthew's ambition, she went to Adrianople to

---

[9] Nicol, *Byzantine Family of Kantakouzenos*, pp. 64–5.   [10] Gregoras, II, pp. 788–9.

[11] A. Tsakopoulos, Περιγραφικὸς Κατάλογος τῶν χειρογράφων τῆς βιβλιοθήκης τοῦ Οἰκουμενικοῦ Πατριαρχείου, II: Ἁγ. Τριάδος Χαλκῆς (Istanbul, 1956), p. 55.

reason with him and restrain him.[12] Trouble there was to be. Eirene did her best to forestall it and to alleviate it when it came. Any jealousy that she may have encountered from the senior Empress Anna of Savoy was relieved when, in 1351, Anna decided that she would rather live in Thessalonica and left Constantinople for good. She reigned there as Empress in her own right until her death as a nun in 1365–6.[13]

Eirene persuaded her son Matthew to sink his pride, at least for a while. He was rewarded with the gift of an appanage in Thrace. When she got back to Constantinople, however, Eirene learnt of the death of her youngest son Andronikos. He was no more than fourteen years old. He was a victim of the Black Death which swept through Byzantium in 1347. It was no consolation to her to be told that God was punishing her for her adherence to the heretical doctrine of Gregory Palamas.[14] It was probably against her nature to do so. The mystical theology of Palamas and the hesychasts was not much favoured by the aristocratic ladies and nuns of the time.[15] But Eirene had to follow the lead of her husband who firmly believed that their theology was correct and supported Palamas as a personal friend. Eirene could never believe that her husband could do any wrong. In the summer of the following year 1348 he called upon her again to prove her ability and courage. He had left her in charge of the administration and defence of Constantinople while he went off on campaign against the Bulgarians. Her second son Manuel was with her as well as her son-in-law Nikephoros, who had married her daughter Maria. Her husband was taken seriously ill. His return was delayed. The Genoese, from their colony at Galata across the Golden Horn, saw their moment to strike at Constantinople. They were angry and alarmed that the new Emperor had taken measures to curtail their lucrative trade in Byzantine waters and to rebuild the Byzantine navy. In August 1348 they sailed across from Galata and set fire to all the new ships that they could find.

Eirene rose to the occasion, as she had done before at Didymoteichon during the civil war. She defied the Genoese and refused to negotiate with their leaders. She had the backing of the citizens; and her son and son-in-law, though still young, ably defended the walls of the city

[12] Gregoras, II, pp. 805–13. Gregoras here invents a long speech reportedly made by Eirene.

[13] On Anna of Savoy, see below, pp. 82–95.

[14] Gregoras, II, pp. 825–6. On Andronikos Cantacuzene, see Nicol, Byzantine Family of Kantakouzenos, no. 26.

[15] See G. Weiss, Johannes Kantakuzenos – Aristokrat, Staatsmann, Kaiser und Mönch (Wiesbaden, 1969), pp. 119, 130.

against repeated attacks. 'Such was the feeling in the air', writes the historian Gregoras,

> that everyone helped in the defence [of Constantinople], bringing out weapons and horses. Builders, tailors and metal workers, all took to arms; and labourers and navvies who enlisted as mercenaries found themselves handling oars and taking to the sea. Even slaves were given weapons by their masters and taught themselves the use of bows and arrows. For the unexpected crisis goaded everyone on to eagerness.[16]

The Genoese were surprised at the strength of the resistance. They had to withdraw with many casualties and again sent ambassadors to negotiate. Still the Empress Eirene refused to talk to them. She would defend the city to the last drop of her blood but she would not treat with the enemy without the permission of her husband. She was, as ever, the dutiful wife, and when he returned from Thrace on 1 October 1348 he commended her steadfastness. He too refused to be browbeaten by the Genoese. Events were to prove that he might have been wiser to give them a chance to talk, for the skirmishing developed into open war. In 1349 the newly constructed Byzantine ships which he had ordered were soon scuttled by the superior seamanship of the Italians; and he was obliged to make a not very favourable treaty of peace. Many blamed him for it, but no one blamed his courageous wife for doing what she conceived to be her duty in a time of crisis.[17]

It was in her well-meaning efforts to mediate between her son Matthew and her son-in-law John Palaiologos that she failed. The danger grew that they would come to blows over their respective rights and precipitate another round of civil war over the succession to the throne. Matthew remained loyal and obedient to his father's wishes until the time came when he felt that his brother-in-law's insolence had gone too far. As a last resort Eirene, at the request of her husband, tried again to act as a peacemaker. She took with her a delegation of three bishops to lend moral weight to her persuasion. This time she had no success. Neither party would sign any agreement; and within the year war had broken out between the two.[18] As his mother, Eirene no doubt had more sympathy for Matthew; and had she been a different woman she might have taken his side. But as always she was committed to her husband's plans and policies and he was not yet ready to declare his son Matthew to be heir to his throne by disinheriting his son-in-law John Palaiologos. John Cantacuzene was never one to take quick decisions

---

[16] Gregoras, II, pp. 850–1.   [17] Nicol, *Last Centuries*, pp. 221–7.
[18] Gregoras, III, pp. 152–71; Cantacuzene, III, pp. 239–41.

until circumstances forced them on him. By the end of 1352, however, Matthew had gained the upper hand in the contest, driving his rival out of Thrace to take refuge on the island of Tenedos. From there, in March 1353, he tried to force the issue by sailing across to break into Constantinople. The Emperor was not there at the time; and once again it was Eirene who took command. The attempt failed. But it was this event which finally induced the Emperor John Cantacuzene to come to a decision. Yielding to the demands of his senators and officers in the capital, and perhaps also to the pleas of his wife, he agreed that Matthew should now be acknowledged and proclaimed as Emperor and heir to the throne in place of John Palaiologos. He was not crowned as such until February 1354, for the Patriarch Kallistos declined to perform the ceremony and preferred to resign rather than to sanction what he thought to be an illegal act.[19]

There were now three Emperors and four Empresses in a world in which God had ordained that there should be only one of each. For Matthew followed the custom of crowning his wife after his coronation. Such an arrangement was doomed to fail. The popularity of John Cantacuzene as the senior Emperor sank to its lowest ebb when, in March 1354, the Turks, his supposed friends and allies, occupied Gallipoli and for the first time established themselves on European soil. There was a strong feeling in favour of a change in government. On the night of 21–22 November John Palaiologos slipped over from Tenedos with a few ships and, with the help of friends and supporters, sneaked into Constantinople. He was welcomed as the true Emperor. John Cantacuzene could do no more. He elected to throw in the sponge rather than fight it out. After some hesitation he agreed to abdicate and to fulfil what he claimed had long been his secret wish by entering a monastery. On 10 December at a ceremony in the palace he divested himself of his imperial insignia and took on the habit of a monk, adopting the monastic name of Joasaph. He retired to the monastery of St George of the Mangana in Constantinople.[20]

He had talked the matter over with Eirene, but she had little option. She had to part from her husband. If and when a married man chose to become a monk, it was normal practice for his wife to become a nun. Eirene may have argued with him, thinking about the succession of her son Matthew, already crowned as Emperor. It has been suggested that she may even have tried to play the part of Justinian's Theodora by

[19] Nicol, *Byzantine Family of Kantakouzenos*, pp. 113–14.
[20] *Ibid.*, pp. 114–15. On the revised chronology of these events, see A. Failler, 'Nouvelle note sur la chronologie du règne de Jean Cantacuzène', *REB*, xxxiv (1976), 119–24.

stiffening his resolve to continue the fight instead of losing his nerve and tamely giving in. She could have rebuked him by saying, 'If I had guarded Didymoteichon as you have guarded Constantinople we should have said our farewells twelve years ago.'[21] It was not her style to argue with her husband, however; and she must have known that the actions of his Turkish allies had lost him what little popularity he had among his subjects. He himself is on record as saying that she had for some years shared his own intention to retreat into the monastic life.[22] Eirene was to the end the dutiful wife. She accepted his decision without protest. On 11 December she too left the palace and, exchanging the vestments of an Empress for the habit of a nun, she retired to the fashionable convent of Kyra Martha, taking the monastic name of Eugenia.[23]

She had been right to be apprehensive about her son Matthew. It had been agreed that he should continue to reign with the title of Emperor over an autonomous 'Empire' in Thrace. He was not satisfied with this fiction, and he was soon goaded into war by his rival John Palaiologos. It was not until December 1357 that, after various adventures, Matthew was persuaded to renounce his imperial title and to swear an oath of allegiance to his rival, thenceforth the sole Emperor of Constantinople. Eirene, who had refused to be implicated in a plot on Matthew's behalf, attended the oath-taking ceremony in the presence of the Patriarch at Epibatai on the Bosporos. For once the agreement was conclusive. At last there was only one Emperor and one Empress. Neither Matthew nor any other member of the Cantacuzene family ever again aspired to the throne. He seems to have lived privately in Constantinople until in 1361, perhaps because of another visitation of the plague, he went with his father and mother to stay with his younger brother Manuel in the Peloponnese. There he stayed until his death some thirty years later. Eirene and her husband returned to Constantinople in 1362 and settled down again in their respective retreats. The date of Eirene's death is not recorded. She was still alive in April 1363, but she seems to have been dead before 1379. She was therefore fortunate enough not to live through the next Byzantine palace revolution when her elderly husband

---

[21] The statement is invented for her by V. Parisot, *Cantacuzène homme d'état et historien* (Paris, 1845), p. 298.
[22] Cantacuzene, III, pp. 106–7.
[23] The convent of Kyra Martha had been founded by Maria, the nun Martha, sister of Michael VIII. The mortal remains of Eirene's mother-in-law Theodora, who died as a prisoner during the civil war, were buried there after 1347, R. Janin, *La géographie ecclésiastique*, pp. 324–6.

and other members of her family were taken hostage by the rebellious Andronikos IV.[24]

The happiest period of Eirene's life was in the years of her husband's reign as Emperor in Constantinople. She was so relieved at his safe return to her after all the fighting and so thrilled by his victory that she wanted the facts to be commemorated for evermore. He had entered Constantinople as Emperor on the night of 2 February 1347. It was the Feast of the Purification of the Virgin, the Feast of Light. Eirene commissioned Nikephoros Gregoras and some other literati to compose speeches of thanks to the Mother of God for having made her husband's victory possible so that the event could be remembered every year at a thanksgiving service. The text of Gregoras's composition has survived. Much of it is written as though it were from the mouth of Eirene herself. It is a stylised exercise in Byzantine rhetoric, but it has its moving moments. She hails the day of her husband's victory as a sweet spring after the long winter of her tearful melancholy. She recalls how, during his absence, she could do no more than mourn the fate of her children, suffering as they were in captivity, or lost in an alien and unknown land. The intercession of the Virgin has transformed her winter into spring and her sadness into joy.[25]

Her thanksgiving speech was probably never read. It certainly never became the central point of the annual celebration of an event which even ten years later had been overtaken by other events in the political turmoil of fourteenth-century Byzantium. The Virgin had doubtless been a comfort to Eirene in the lonely and uncertain years of her isolation during the civil war. But Gregoras was wise to conclude his speech with his own prayer to her beseeching her to continue to watch over her people, her flock, seeing the storms and waves lashing their city, their enemies already trampling its forecourts, while all around they were already prisoners-of-war. Eirene had been a brave woman and a faithful and courageous defender of her husband's cause. He himself accorded her the highest accolade that a Byzantine man could ever bring himself to grant to a woman of spirit, that she had many manly virtues. She was endowed with talents and intelligence greater than the feminine norm.[26] But it is the historian and polymath Gregoras who more often extols the strength of her character, for all that her

[24] Nicol, *Last Centuries*, pp. 249–50.
[25] L. G. Westerink, 'Nikephoros Gregoras, Dankrede an die Mutter Gottes', *Helikon*, VII (1967), 259–71 (reprinted in Westerink, *Texts and Studies in Neoplatonism and Byzantine Literature* (Amsterdam, 1980), pp. 229–41). H.-V. Beyer, 'Eine Chronologie der Lebensgeschichte des Nikephoros Gregoras', *JÖB*, XXVII (1978), 137.
[26] Cantacuzene, II, p. 336; III, p. 49.

husband had led her astray in theology.[27] It turned out that Gregoras was behind the times in pursuing his vendetta against the doctrine of Palamas. It was Eirene's husband who, as Emperor, presided over the synod which declared that doctrine to be true. In this too she was on the side of the angels. Eirene, the nun Eulogia, is to this day numbered among the pious Empresses of immortal memory in the Synodikon of Orthodoxy, the liturgical document which records the champions of the true faith. It is a clear indication that she followed her husband's lead in matters of religion as in everything else.[28]

[27] Gregoras, II, pp. 625, 692, 805.
[28] J. Gouillard, 'Le Synodikon de l'Orthodoxie. Edition et commentaire', TM, II (1967), 103. It has been proposed that Eirene, as wife of John Cantacuzene, is one of the two Empresses depicted on a small ivory pyxis in Dumbarton Oaks. But the identification of the figures on this object is far from certain. A. Grabar, 'Une pyxide en ivoire à Dumbarton Oaks. Quelques notes sur l'art profane pendant les derniers siècles de l'Empire byzantin', DOP, XIV (1960), 121–46.

------ ❦❧ ------

CHAPTER SEVEN

ANNA OF SAVOY,
REGENT AND EMPRESS,
1341–c. 1365

ANNA OF SAVOY, like Yolanda of Montferrat, was a westerner who became a Byzantine by marriage. She was born at Chambéry about 1306, a daughter of Amadeo V Count of Savoy and his wife Maria of Brabant. In the west she was known as Joanna or Giovanna, the name that her parents had given her. Her father Amadeo died in October 1323 and she was left an orphan under the care of her half-brother Edward, Count of Savoy. No one could have foreseen that she would become Empress of Constantinople and deeply involved in the destiny of the Byzantine Empire.

At the time of her father's death the Empire was governed by an uneasy coalition of two emperors, Andronikos III Palaiologos and his grandfather Andronikos II, who had temporarily disinherited him. The quarrel between grandson and grandfather was, again temporarily, patched up in 1325. Andronikos III's first wife had just died. She too had been a westerner, Adelheid-Eirene of Brunswick. She died childless. The future of the ruling family of Byzantium suggested that the younger Emperor, Andronikos III, should marry again and produce an heir to the throne. It was decided that Joanna of Savoy, daughter of the late Count Amadeo, would make a suitable bride. In the summer of 1325 ambassadors were sent from Constantinople to Savoy. They were Andronikos Tornikes, an experienced diplomat of the Byzantine court, and Jean de Gibelet, a relative of the French ruling family of Cyprus and an officer in the Byzantine army. They were graciously received and escorted with a guard of honour to put their proposal to Count Edward and his half-sister Joanna. They were not the first in the line of suitors for the lady's hand, for King Charles IV of France had already inspected her at a bride-show in Paris. The Greek account of the matter has it that the King of France was upstaged by the Emperor of Constantinople; for, as the writer smugly observes, 'the barbarians as well as the Italians and other western rulers still rated marriage into the Byzantine imperial family the highest of all possible matches'. A contract was drafted and signed in September 1325; and about the end of November Joanna of Savoy, henceforth to be known as Anna, left her ancestral home in Italy never to return.[1]

She was escorted on her voyage from Savona by her chaplain, three Franciscan friars, and a retinue of Savoyard knights, esquires and ladies in waiting. The Byzantines were much impressed and staged a grand reception for her and her company when they reached Constantinople in February 1326. But it had been a long and difficult journey for her in the middle of winter and Anna succumbed to an illness as soon as she arrived. Her wedding had to be postponed. It was not until October that she was fit enough for the ceremony. It was performed in Constantinople probably by the Patriarch according to the Byzantine rite, a fact which much annoyed the Pope. In his view marriages between Catholics and Orthodox were uncanonical and forbidden unless specifically approved by the papacy. Pope John XXII had not been party to the arrangements made for the marriage of Anna, a pious Catholic princess, to a husband who, however exalted, was in schism from the one true church. Count Edward of Savoy, to whom the Pope wrote an angry letter, replied rather feebly and without much conviction that Anna might convert her husband.[2] It seems unlikely that she ever tried. She was never given to profundities. There are many signs that she missed the western way of life and enjoyed the company of her Italian knights and ladies. But she wanted to please her husband. She

---

[1] The most exhaustive documented biography of Anna of Savoy is that by D. Muratore, *Una principessa Sabauda sul trono di Bisanzio. Giovanna di Savoia Imperatrice Anna Paleologina* (Mémoires de l'Académie des sciences, belles-lettres et arts de Savoie, 4th ser., xi) (Chambéry, 1909), pp. 221–475. See also C. Diehl, 'Anne de Savoie, femme d'Andronic III', *Figures byzantines*, ii (Paris, 1921), pp. 245–65 (= Diehl, *Impératrices de Byzance* (Paris, 1959), pp. 275–95); *PLP*, ix, no. 21437. John Cantacuzene, *History*, ed. L. Schopen (*CSHB* 1828–32), i, pp. 193–6, 204–5, gives a very full account of the circumstances of her marriage. It is probable that an intermediary in the negotiations between Savoy and Constantinople was Theodore, Marquis of Montferrat, son of Andronikos II and Yolanda, who was on one of his rare visits to Constantinople in 1325. The houses of Savoy and Montferrat were connected by blood and by political interest. See Angeliki E. Laiou, *Constantinople and the Latins. The Foreign Policy of Andronicus II, 1282–1328* (Cambridge, Mass., 1972), pp. 302–5 (cited below as Laiou, *Andronicus II*); Ursula V. Bosch, *Kaiser Andronikos III. Palaiologos* (Amsterdam, 1965), pp. 36, 106–7.

[2] Letter of Pope John XXII, ed. A. L. Tautu, *Acta Ioannis XXII (1317–1334)* (Vatican City, 1952), no. 141a (31 December 1325). J. Gill, *Byzantium and the Papacy* (New Brunswick, N.J., 1979), pp. 240–1; Muratore, *Una principessa Sabauda*, pp. 253–4; Laiou, *Andronicus II*, p. 304.

learnt to speak his language and she adopted his form of the Christian faith.

Immediately after her wedding her husband the Emperor placed a crown upon her head according to Byzantine custom and she became his Empress as well as his wife, no longer Anna of Savoy but Anna Palaiologina. Most of her Savoyard knights and ladies who had accompanied her to Constantinople left for home when the ceremonies were over. One, however, stayed with her as her principal lady in waiting for another twenty years. She was Isabella de la Rochette, known to the Greeks as Zampea.[3] Some of the knights also stayed since they got on so well with Anna's husband. He was intrigued by the western arts of horsemanship to which they introduced him. Some of them were his guests in the palace and went hunting with him; and they taught him the martial arts of jousting and tournaments, though they were not the first to introduce such sports to the Byzantine court as he seemed to think. The young Andronikos clearly enjoyed them; and he invited other knights to come to Constantinople every year to stage joustings and tournaments in which he took part. The older members of his court expressed some disapproval at their Emperor's frivolity and feared that he was putting himself at bodily risk by throwing himself into these foreign and barbarous activities.[4]

Anna spent the first years of her marriage at Didymoteichon in Thrace, perhaps because the air of the countryside was better for her health than that of Constantinople. It was at Didymoteichon on 18 June 1332 that she gave birth to the first of her sons. He was called John. She had fulfilled the purpose of her marriage by producing an heir to the throne. He was later to be known as John V Palaiologos the Emperor. By the time that he was born the unseemly squabble over possession of the throne was at an end. Anna's husband had forced his elderly grandfather to abdicate and had become sole Emperor in May 1328. Anna was thus Empress in fact as well as in name. So long as her husband was alive, however, she played little part in the government of his Empire and he preferred to take his advice from his Grand Domestic or commander-in-chief and lifelong friend, John Cantacuzene. She kept him well supplied with children, however. About 1327 she bore him a daughter, Eirene Palaiologina who, at the tender age of five, was betrothed to the fifteen-year old son of the Tsar of Bulgaria, John Asen.[5] In

---

[3] *PLP*, III, no. 6446.   [4] Cantacuzene, I, pp. 204–5; Gregoras, I, pp. 482–3.
[5] Cantacuzene, I, p. 394 (who wrongly calls her Maria); Gregoras, I, p. 546. A. Th. Papadopulos, *Versuch einer Genealogie der Palaiologen 1259–1453* (Munich, 1938; repr. Amsterdam, 1962), no. 77.

1337 Anna produced a second son called Michael Palaiologos who, though styled as a Porphyrogenitus and ennobled as a Despot, seldom made his name in history.[6] She also had two other daughters: Maria Palaiologina, who married the Genoese Lord of Lesbos Francesco I Gattilusio; and Theodora Palaiologina.[7] It was on her elder son John Palaiologos, however, that Anna relied in the event of any constitutional crisis.

The first crisis occurred in 1330. In January her husband the Emperor was taken gravely ill while at Didymoteichon. He was near death and his doctors despaired of curing him. He made a miraculous recovery, however, and was soon able to return to his duties in Constantinople.[8] The second crisis came in 1341 when Anna's husband was again smitten with illness which seemed to have no cure. He died on the night of 14–15 June. Anna was suddenly left a widow with her two little sons John aged nine and Michael aged four. Nikephoros Gregoras composed a lament for her, addressing her as 'divine Empress'. It is a pedantic rhetorical exercise. But he rightly and with sympathy describes her cruel loss as a storm which had shattered the vernal harmony of her life.[9] She was lonely and fearful for her children. She had little experience in the way the Empire was run. She had never had to take decisions on war or peace. She quickly found that there were several able and ambitious men at hand ready to advise and help her organise a regency for herself and her son John until he came of age. Foremost among them was John Cantacuzene, her late husband's closest friend, comrade-in-arms and counsellor. It was he who took her children under his wing during the last hours of her husband's life and secured them under guard of the Varangian troops in the palace in case there might be trouble.[10] In the weeks after her husband's funeral in 1341 Cantacuzene acted as though he were in fact regent of the Empire and guardian of the lawful heir John and his mother Anna. There was justice in his claim. When the late Emperor Andronikos had been at death's door in 1330 he had personally nominated his friend Cantacuzene as guardian and protector of the Empress Anna. He was not alone in assuming that the Emperor had not changed his mind. But in 1341 there were others in the running for the office of regent, notably the Patriarch of Constantinople, John

[6] *PLP*, IX, no. 21521.
[7] Papadopulos, *Genealogie*, nos. 78, 79. Papadopulos, no. 76, lists Theodore Palaiologos the *protovestiarios* as a third son of Anna and Andronikos III. But see *PLP*, IX, no. 21461.
[8] Cantacuzene, I, pp. 391–411, 426–7; Gregoras, I, pp. 439–40.
[9] Cantacuzene, I, pp. 557–60; Gregoras, I, pp. 559–65.
[10] Cantacuzene, I, pp. 559–60.

Kalekas, and an able but unscrupulous upstart called Alexios Apokaukos, who owed what fame and fortune he had acquired to John Cantacuzene. He now turned against his benefactor and supported the claim of the Patriarch to act as regent along with the Empress Anna. The Patriarch too had some justice on his side, for he had twice before taken over the reins of government when Andronikos III and Cantacuzene had been away on campaigns; and he was a cleric of a worldly turn of mind.[11]

Anna, as Dowager Empress, was at the mercy of ambitious and pretentious men, all protesting that their prime and innocent concern was the protection of herself and her family and especially the right of her son John to inherit his late father's throne and title when he came to maturity. She was over thirty years of age. She had borne five children. She had lived, albeit in the comfort of palaces, among Greek-speakers for half her life. She had embraced the Orthodox faith. Yet she preferred the company of her Italian ladies in waiting and she must have found it hard to comprehend or to trust the devious minds and specious arguments of the men of Constantinople who surrounded her in her widowhood. She was genuinely grateful to John Cantacuzene for his solicitude and support in her hour of need. But she was not sure that she could trust him; she may often have been jealous of his special relationship and friendship with her husband; and she had ambitions of her own. In one of his conversations with the Patriarch before the crisis came to a head, Cantacuzene remarked that while he was convinced of the Empress's sincerity, he feared for her natural weakness as a woman. He quoted a 'Persian' proverb to the effect that, though a woman's head might reach the clouds yet she remained on earth, signifying that for all her qualities of magnanimity and courage she could not rise above her inherent feebleness as the weaker sex. Anna seemed determined to challenge this banal truism.[12]

The storm broke in September 1341 when Cantacuzene left Constantinople to perform his military duties in Thrace. As soon as he was gone his political opponents, led, bribed, or flattered by Alexios Apokaukos, whipped up support for the formation of a regency composed of the Patriarch John Kalekas and the Empress Anna. The Patriarch needed no persuading that he was effectively its head. Anna was induced to sign an order for Cantacuzene to resign his command and disband his army. He remained convinced that right was on his side. The issue was to be resolved by another round of civil war, more devastating in its

[11] D. M. Nicol, *The Byzantine Family of Kantakouzenos* pp. 47–8.
[12] Cantacuzene, II, pp. 47–8.

consequences than any that the Byzantines had ever brought upon themselves. Apokaukos saw to it that Cantacuzene was denounced as a traitor set upon seizing the throne for himself. His associates and members of his own family were arrested and their property in Constantinople was seized. The Empress Anna, now recognized as regent for her son, at first refused to believe the accusations hurled at her late husband's best friend. The worst seemed to be confirmed when, in October 1341, Cantacuzene allowed himself to be proclaimed Emperor in Thrace by his troops and political supporters, many of them refugees from the terror in Constantinople.[13]

The civil war which then broke out was to last for nearly six years, until in February 1347 Cantacuzene righted the wrongs done to him by entering Constantinople as Emperor. During those years Anna Palaiologina, once a young princess of Savoy, came of age as guardian of the throne for her son John and also as a woman of the world, an Empress playing the part of an Emperor. It had happened in times past. The formidable Empress Eirene at the end of the eighth century had liked to be known as Emperor in the masculine gender. But Anna was not her equal and she was out of her depth in a sea of opportunist male colleagues and advisers, notably the devious Alexios Apokaukos and his friends. In November 1341, less than a month after Cantacuzene's proclamation as Emperor in Thrace, she was persuaded to have her son John crowned as Emperor in Constantinople. He was not yet ten years old, but his coronation was performed with righteous propriety by the Patriarch, who had just, with equally righteous fervour, excommunicated the 'usurper' Cantacuzene, the rival contender for the crown.[14]

The regency of the Empress Anna and the Patriarch John between 1341 and 1347 was a catastrophic interlude in Byzantine history. Neither knew much about statecraft, diplomacy, or finances, still less of how to conduct a civil war against a determined adversary. The economy of the Empire ran down; the Byzantine gold coinage, once the only stable currency in the Christian world, had to be devalued and depreciated to the point of worthlessness. The Italian Republics of Venice and Genoa, the exploiters of the wealth of Constantinople, made the most of the Empress's embarrassment. For she remembered that she was herself Italian and looked to them for moral support and economic aid. In September 1341 she made a new treaty with the Republic of Genoa, thus healing the rift between Constantinople and the Genoese merchants at Galata across the Golden Horn. In March 1342 she

[13] Nicol, *Byzantine Family of Kantakouzenos*, pp. 47–8.
[14] Gregoras, II, pp. 614–16; Cantacuzene, II, pp. 190, 218.

renewed the long-standing Byzantine treaty with Venice which had lapsed after ten years. Both of these treaty documents were purportedly in the names of Anna and her son, though little John Palaiologos can hardly have understood them.[15] In August of the same year she tried to tempt the Serbian Tsar Stephen Dušan, who had befriended Cantacuzene, into handing him over dead or alive. His reward would be a generous extension of Serbian territories in Thrace. Even Dušan was shocked. She likewise tried to bring over the Tsar of Bulgaria.[16] In the spring of 1343 she sent one of her Savoyard knights, Giovanni d'Orlay, to Venice to ask the senators to use their influence to stop Dušan from supporting Cantacuzene.[17] She also asked for their help against the ever-encroaching Turks. Yet she had already been appealing to the Turks to come across the Hellespont as mercenaries and allies to fight on her behalf. It made matters no better that her adversary did the same. One of the consequences of the disastrous civil war was the settlement of the Turks in Europe. Whoever won that war the Turks would be the beneficiaries.[18]

As her inventiveness and resources began to run out, Anna made two extravagant gestures. She sent one of her knights, Philip of Saint Germain, with two Franciscans from Galata, bearing letters to Pope Clement VI at Avignon. She seems to have worn her religious beliefs rather lightly. She must have known that the papacy had disapproved of her marriage to a heretic and no doubt also of the Orthodox baptism and coronation of her son John. In the summer of 1343, when she wrote to him, Pope Clement VI had been in office for barely a year. He was much concerned about the victories of the Turks in the eastern Mediterranean and had in mind the formation of a league of Christian powers against them.[19] But he did not feel so strongly about the internecine conflict between the ruling families of Constantinople which they had evidently brought upon themselves. Anna hoped to win his favour and support by proposing her reversion to her childhood obedience to the Holy See and the conversion to Catholicism of her son John. She also told the Pope that the other regents of her Empire, Alexios Apokaukos and the Patriarch of Constantinople, were eager to make the same sub-

---

[15] *DR*, v, nos. 2864, 2876. [16] *DR*, v, nos. 2879–81, 2892.

[17] *DR*, v, no. 2888.

[18] Cantacuzene, (II, p. 506) claimed that it was Anna and not he who had been the first to call on the help of the Turks. Certainly she did so on five occasions between 1344 and 1346. *DR*, v, nos. 1895, 2902–3, 2904, 2906, 2912. N. Jorga, 'Latins et grecs d'Orient et l'établissement des Turcs en Europe, 1342–62', *BZ*, xv (1906), 179–222.

[19] J. Gay, *Le pape Clément VI et les affaires d'Orient (1342–1352)* (Paris, 1904), pp. 33–4, 45–9; K. M. Setton, *The Papacy and the Levant (1204–1571)*, I, pp. 189f.

mission, as were the monks of Mount Athos. John V would have done whatever his mother told him to do. But nothing appears less probable than the conversion to Catholicism of Apokaukos, the Patriarch, or the monks of Athos. The text of these letters is lost. Their alleged content is known only from the Pope's replies to Anna and her son in October 1343.[20]

There is something curious about this affair. Anna may have been naive. But she was surely not so stupid as to pretend that the Patriarch of Constantinople, her fellow regent, was willing to go over to the Roman church. Years later John Cantacuzene in his Memoirs claimed that Anna's letters to Pope Clement were forged by the ingenious Apokaukos who had by then seen his way to achieving his real purpose, to discredit and eliminate Anna and her son and seize the throne for himself. For he knew that 'there was nothing so calculated to rouse the Byzantine people to wrath and bloody revolution as the news that their Empress had embraced the Latin faith'. John Cantacuzene is perhaps too often accused of weighting his evidence to his own advantage. In this case he may well have been right.[21]

Anna's second extravagant gesture was with regard to Venice. She had renewed Byzantium's trade agreement with the Republic in 1342. A year later, when the Empire's resources were at a still lower ebb, she begged for a substantial loan. The Venetians knew well enough the facts of her economic plight. They knew that she would probably never be able to repay them. They made sure therefore that the conditions of the loan were carefully defined and that the interest on it and security for it must be correspondingly substantial. In August 1343 Anna caused her son John to put his sign or signature to a promissory note and, through the good offices of the Venetian baillie in Constantinople, the transaction was completed. Anna and her government were the richer by a loan from Venice of 30,000 ducats. She was reckless in her hopes and promises. As security she made over the crown jewels of Byzantium. She pledged to repay the loan within three years at a rate of 10,000 ducats a year with interest at 5 per cent. It was a transaction made without thought of the consequences. The loan was never repaid in full. The interest mounted as the years went on. The affair was a bone of

[20] P. Lemerle, *L'Emirat d'Aydin, Byzance et l'Occident* (Paris, 1957), pp. 160–1, 182–3. Clement VI, *Letters*, ed. E. Déprez, *Clément VI (1342–1352), Lettres closes, patentes et curiales publiées ou analysées d'après les registres du Vatican* (Paris, 1901–1925), I, nos. 466–71 (all dated 21 October 1343).
[21] Cantacuzene, II, pp. 539–41. *Letters of Clement VI*, ed. Déprez, I, no. 493 (to Alexios Apokaukos: dated 27 October 1343); *DR*, v, no. 2890. Lemerle, *L'Emirat d'Aydin*, p. 183 n. 1.

contention between Venice and Constantinople until the end of the Empire; and the crown jewels remained in the Treasury of St Mark's at least until the Turks conquered Constantinople in 1453.[22]

In the fourteenth century the Venetian ducat was worth about two of the debased gold coins of Byzantium. With her new-found riches Anna, goaded on by her advisers, felt that she could persevere until her adversary was forced to give in. He too was hard pressed for cash to pay his mercenaries and allies. But gradually the tide turned in his favour as people saw that Constantinople as well as the northern provinces were being devastated and impoverished by senseless warfare. Many of Anna's supporters changed sides; many were imprisoned for trying to do so; many of those who still had wealth took refuge with the Genoese at Galata across the water from Constantinople. The money from Venice soon disappeared, much of it no doubt into the pockets of Alexios Apokaukos, who took to feathering his nest and preparing his refuge beyond the city in case the political wind changed. Anna was reduced to selling the silver from icons in the churches. She became more and more ruthless. People trying to escape from the terror in Constantinople were denied the sacred right of asylum in the church of St Sophia and were incarcerated in the new dungeon which Apokaukos had built for political prisoners. Secret agents were sent out on eight occasions to assassinate Cantacuzene either by poison or by the sword.[23] The Patriarch began to doubt Anna's judgment. He confessed that, in his view, the real cause of all the evils of the time was simply jealousy – the jealousy of Anna for Cantacuzene and his loyal and courageous wife Eirene who also claimed the title of Empress. It was the opinion of Gregoras as a contemporary historian that Anna, as well as being jealous, was unbalanced and incompetent and could not tell right from wrong. Her only loyalty was to her son John. These defects he ascribes, in the fashion of his time, to the facts that she was a woman and of foreign extraction as well. A later historian has it that Anna, as a woman, ruled like a malfunctioning weaver's shuttle that ripped and distorted the purple cloth of empire.[24]

In June 1345 Alexios Apokaukos was murdered by some of his political prisoners. Anna lost her most efficient and dangerous supporter. Still she refused to give in. She was furious when she discovered that the

---

[22] D. M. Nicol, *Byzantium and Venice. A study in diplomatic and cultural relations* (Cambridge, 1988), pp. 258–60.

[23] Cantacuzene, II, pp. 489, 558–63, 589–90, 597–8.

[24] Gregoras, II, pp. 748–51, 760–1; Doukas, *Istoria Turco-Bizantină* ed. V. Grecu (Bucharest, 1958), p. 47.

Patriarch had been in secret correspondence with Cantacuzene suggesting that a peace settlement should be arranged.[25] She felt that the time had come to be rid of him. This could best be done by having him condemned and deposed by a vote of his bishops on theological grounds. Anna herself hardly understood what those grounds were; but she gladly embraced the cause of the Patriarch's theological opponents and thereby secured his condemnation and dismissal at a hastily convened synod in Constantinople. She was then regent on her own.[26]

It was too late. On the night after the synod, on 2 February 1347, Cantacuzene fought his way into the city. He drew up his troops outside the walls of the palace. Anna barricaded herself inside and refused to talk to the messengers that he sent her. Her stubbornness was partly inspired by apprehension. She had convinced herself that she and her son were now about to be arrested and imprisoned if not worse. Some of Cantacuzene's officers finally lost patience and anticipated their orders by storming their way into the palace. Anna then at last submitted and sent representatives to make peace. On 8 February a settlement was arranged. Its terms were such that it might well have been reached six years earlier. It was agreed that John Cantacuzene and the young John Palaiologos, now about fifteen years old, should reign together as colleagues, the former being recognised as senior Emperor for the space of ten years, after which they would reign jointly. Cantacuzene promised to take no reprisals and to bear no malice against Anna and her son. All political prisoners were to be released and the immediate past was, so far as possible, to be forgotten. Men marvelled at the contrast between the magnanimity of John Cantacuzene in his hour of triumph and the pusillanimity of the Empress Anna. There were those who saw the dawning of a new era after the long years of civil war.[27]

Part of the settlement was that Anna's son John was to marry Helena, Cantacuzene's youngest daughter, who was fourteen. The marriage was celebrated in May 1347 by the new Patriarch of Constantinople after he had crowned Cantacuzene as the senior Emperor John VI. In theory there were now two Emperors, a senior and a junior, and two Empresses, Anna and Eirene, Cantacuzene's wife. It looked well on paper but it was doomed to failure in practice. Anna and Eirene could not easily live as equals in the same city. Nor could Eirene's own son Matthew Cantacuzene be content to play second fiddle to Anna's son

[25] Gregoras, II, p. 767.
[26] J. Meyendorff, *Introduction à l'étude de Grégoire Palamas* (Paris, 1959), pp. 117–19.
[27] D. M. Nicol, *The Last Centuries of Byzantium, 1261–1453* (Cambridge, 1993), pp. 206–8.

John. The senior Emperor hoped to prevent trouble by sending John to reside as Emperor in Thessalonica. It was a mistake, for there the young man found supporters who encouraged him to resume the fight against the 'usurper' Cantacuzene and his family. Among them was the Serbian Stephen Dušan who saw profit to be made in posing as champion of the junior Emperor. It was a dangerous situation, for Dušan had recently proclaimed himself as yet another Emperor and his sights were set not only on Thessalonica but on Constantinople as well.

In the summer of 1351 the Serbians were already encamped at the gates of Thessalonica. Cantacuzene could not leave his capital. He prevailed on Anna to go for him, to prevent disaster and to reprimand her son. She rose to the occasion. She told her son not to be so foolish. She harangued his partisans. She went to call on Stephen Dušan in his camp outside the walls of Thessalonica and persuaded him to withdraw.[28] It was a considerable diplomatic achievement; and it marks the beginning of a new phase in Anna's career. She never went back to Constantinople. For some fourteen years she reigned as Empress over what was described as her own 'portion' of Empire in Thessalonica. Her son John left there early in 1352 to reside in his independent imperial appanage in Thrace; and there before long he was at war with Cantacuzene's son Matthew. It was the end of the settlement so hopefully made between the warring factions of the houses of Palaiologos and Cantacuzene in 1347. The last phase of their feud culminated in 1354 in the abdication of John Cantacuzene and the triumph of Anna's son John V Palaiologos, who at last became unchallenged Emperor of the Romans.[29]

No doubt Anna was pleased and gratified that her long struggle on behalf of her son's rights had not been in vain. She could hardly have done more for him. Now she was happy to manage her own portion of Empire in the smaller world of Thessalonica. She did so with style and dignity, proudly retaining her titles of Augusta and Empress. Other imperial ladies before her had, for different reasons, found Thessalonica more congenial than Constantinople. Eirene of Montferrat, the second wife of Andronikos II, had reigned there from 1303 to 1317, if only to escape from and annoy her husband.[30] The widow of the Emperor Michael IX had retired there in 1320 and spent the last thirteen years of her life in Thessalonica as a somewhat pampered nun. Anna, however found a new fulfilment and sense of purpose in managing her own little Empire from her own imperial palace. She issued her own decrees and

[28] Cantacuzene, III, pp. 200–9; Gregoras, III, p. 149.
[29] Nicol, *Byzantine Family of Kantakouzenos*, pp. 79–87.
[30] See above, pp. 52–7.

ordinances.[31] She minted her own coins. Most of those that survive depict the standing figure of an Emperor on the reverse, who must surely be her son John. Anna herself, however, is shown crowned, in full imperial regalia and bearing a sceptre in her right hand and in her left a model of the battlemented city of Thessalonica. Her portrait is clearly designated by the letter A. People were not to be allowed to forget that their Empress was Anna Palaiologina, the princess from Savoy who became first Empress and regent of Constantinople and then Empress of Thessalonica.[32] A vivid reminder of this fact can still be seen in an inscription carved in a gateway in the acropolis of the city, recording its construction by decree of the Empress (despoina) Anna Palaiologina in 1355.[33] Her last known official act, recorded in a later document, was to make a donation to the convent of the Anargyroi (Cosmas and Damian) in Thessalonica probably in 1360.[34] She died in her city about five years later, as a nun with the name of Anastasia. Her reign there was remembered as an era of peace after the social and political upheavals which had afflicted Thessalonica in the decade before. Nicholas Kabasilas, a native of the city, composed a eulogy of Anna so that the world would know how beneficent was her rule.[35]

It was for long believed, at least by western historians, that she died as an initiate of the third order of Franciscans and was buried at Assisi. This is no more than a pious fiction designed to prove that Anna of Savoy had always been a devoted adherent of the Roman church. She was certainly on good terms with the Franciscans in the Genoese colony at Galata and on occasion employed them as ambassadors to the west. The Popes, evidently half-believing that Anna was still their *filia carissima* in the faith, were fond of quoting to her St Paul's dictum that 'the unbelieving husband can be saved by his wife' (I Cor. VII: 14). It was what her half-brother Edward of Savoy had suggested might happen at

[31] F. Barišić, 'Povelje vizantijskich carica [Les chartes des impératrices byzantines]', *ZRVI*, XIII (1971), 143–202, especially 180–2. On Anna's constitutional position, see Aikaterini Christophilopoulou, Ἡ ἀντιβασιλεία εἰς τὸ Βυζάντιον, Σύμμεικτα, II (1970), 1–144, especially 91–127.

[32] S. Bendall and P. J. Donald, *The Later Palaeologan Coinage* (London, 1979), pp. 248–53; D. Nicol and S. Bendall, 'Anna of Savoy in Thessalonica: the numismatic evidence', *Revue Numismatique*, 6th ser., XIX (1977), 87–102; P. Protonotarios, 'John V and Anna of Savoy (1351 1365). The Serres hoard' (in Greek and English), *Nomismatika Chronika*, VIII (1989), 69–84.

[33] R.-J. Loenertz, 'Chronologie de Nicolas Cabasilas 1345–1354', *OCP*, XXI (1955), 205–31 (= Loenertz, *Byzantina et Franco-Graeca*, I (Rome, 1970), pp. 303–28).

[34] F. Barišić, 'Povelje vizantijskich carica', *ZRVI*, XIII (1971), 181–2. On the convent of the Anargyroi in Thessalonica, see R. Janin, *Les églises et les monastères des grands centres byzantins* (Paris, 1975), p. 350.

[35] Loenertz, 'Chronologie de Nicolas Cabasilas', 320–22 (224–6).

the time of her marriage. There is no sure evidence that it ever did, though a Franciscan chronicler believed that Andronikos III had gone through a form of conversion to the true faith.[36] Anna's modern biographer, Dino Muratore, is too inclined to dwell on her constant loyalty to the Roman church and her nostalgia for her beloved homeland in Savoy.[37] There is little proof of either of these assertions. She could well have gone home after she had successfully installed her son as Emperor in 1354. She preferred to stay in Thessalonica as Empress in her own right; and it was there that she died as a nun of the Orthodox persuasion.

Had she reverted to the Catholic faith of her childhood she would have found it hard to collaborate with the Patriarch of Constantinople during her years as regent of the Empire and still harder to keep the loyalty of her Orthodox subjects; and it is clear from her son's much publicised conversion to Rome in 1369 that his mother had not interfered with his upbringing in the Orthodox faith. Her known benefactions to the church of her adoption reveal that she clung more to the faith of her husband than to that of her fathers. Among the treasures in the monastery of Iviron on Mount Athos is a splendid Psalter written by a well-known scribe of the monastery of the Virgin Hodegetria in Constantinople in 1346. It belonged to 'Anna Palaiologina the Empress', who donated it to that monastery. It was there that her husband had died and there that Anna had kept vigil for him for three days in 1341.[38] Further proof of her impeccable Orthodoxy and of her monastic name of Anastasia is contained in a 'Memorial' of the monastery of the Protaton on Mount Athos, listing the names of secular and ecclesiastical rulers worthy of memory. There she is recorded for all time as 'our Empress Anna of immortal fame known as the nun Anastasia, who in words and deeds laboured all her life in support of the apostolic and patristic dogmas of the church'.[39] This was high praise indeed; and Anna earned it for her politically motivated change of mind when, at the eleventh hour of her regency, she opted to side with the theological opponents of her colleague the Patriarch John Kalekas and secured his deposition as a heretic. It was for this reason if for no other that the Byzantine church bestowed upon her its highest accolade by including her name in the

[36] Muratore, *Una principessa Sabauda*, pp. 462–6; Nicol and Bendall, 'Anna of Savoy in Thessalonica', 93.
[37] See, e.g., Muratore, *Una principessa Sabauda*, pp. 368–9.
[38] L. Politis, 'Eine Schreiberschule im Kloster τῶν Ὁδηγῶν, *BZ*, LI (1958), 263–4.
[39] I. Djurić, 'Pomenik Svetogorskog Protata c kraja XIV veka' (Mémorial du Protaton de Mont Athos à la fin du XIVe siècle), *ZRVI*, xx (1981), 139–61, especially 149–53; Politis, 'Eine Schreiberschule', 274–5.

Synodikon of Orthodoxy as Anna Palaiologina, Empress of blameless and blessed memory.[40]

She led a colourful life. She was frequently out of her depth as regent of Constantinople and given to panic measures. She was consistent and effective only in her championship of her son. In the end, largely thanks to the mistakes of others, she realised her ambition for him when he became sole Emperor in 1354. She then gave herself to her career as Empress in Thessalonica. It was perhaps as well that she died when she did. Her son remained on and off his throne for more than forty years until his death in 1391. He made so many misjudgments and miscalculations that his mother would probably not have been proud of him, for all that she had spent so much of her life in getting him to the throne.

[40] J. Gouillard, 'Le Synodikon de l'Orthodoxie. Edition et commentaire', *TM*, II (1967), 100 3, lines 869 73.

CHAPTER EIGHT

————— ⬦⬦ —————

ANNA NOTARAS PALAIOLOGINA,
DIED 1507

ANNA NOTARAS PALAIOLOGINA lived in a world and an age of change, uncertainty and disruption. She was born and grew up in a privileged and wealthy family of the Byzantine aristocracy when Byzantium was in its terminal decline. She spent most of her adult life as a well-to-do refugee in the flourishing world of early Renaissance Italy. She died in Venice as an elderly spinster in 1507. But she never became acclimatised to the western way of life. It was always her dream to gather round her a protectorate of less fortunate refugees from the wreck of Byzantium to save and perpetuate the language, culture and religion of her Greek-speaking compatriots who had been set adrift from their home and their faith.

Her father Loukas Notaras was one of the rich landed gentry of the Peloponnese, the last of the Byzantine provinces in the fifteenth century.[1] In the course of his distinguished career at the court of the Emperors in Constantinople he had held almost all the high offices of state. In the last years of the Empire he was *mesazon* or prime minister of the last two Emperors, John VIII and his brother, Constantine XI Palaiologos, as well as *megas dux* or Grand Duke. He was esteemed and admired by all, except for the personal friend and adviser of Constantine XI, the historian George Sphrantzes, who was jealous of his influence and his wealth. Loukas Notaras was certainly wealthy; and he had friends in high places among the Italians with whom he had acted as his Emperor's ambassador and interpreter. His many distinctions included honorary citizenship of Venice and of Genoa; and in the dark days before the fall of Constantinople to the Turks in 1453 he had prudently lodged much of his money in Italian banks. Not that he would ever have contemplated deserting the sinking ship of Byzantium and settling in the west.

[1] On the Notaras family, see S. A. Koutibas, Οἱ Νοταράδες στὴν ὑπηρεσία τοῦ ἔθνους καὶ τῆς ἐκκλησίας (Athens, 1968), especially pp. 59–68 (on Anna).

During the long and fatal siege of Constantinople by the Sultan Mehmed II in April and May 1453 Notaras stayed at his post. He went down in history as one of the noblest and bravest defenders of the Christian cause, a hero and a martyr. He is credited with having uttered the memorable statement that he would rather see the Turkish turban in his city than the Latin mitre.[2] Perhaps he did so in a moment of vexation. But it seems out of character for he was a more tolerant Orthodox Christian than many of his fanatically anti-Latin contemporaries; and he numbered members of the Roman Catholic hierarchy among his friends.

He married a lady of the imperial family of Palaiologos, which gave his daughter Anna the right and the excuse to call herself Palaiologina. She was his eldest daughter. He had at least six other children, two girls called Theodora and Euphrosyne, and four sons. The girls are known only from Italian sources, for they too found their way to Italy. One of them married a son of Andronikos Palaiologos, the last Grand Domestic or commander-in-chief of the Byzantine army who was executed by the Turks after the fall of Constantinople.[3] The fate of Loukas Notaras, of his wife and of their sons is famously and dramatically tragic. They were all taken prisoner by the conquering Turks in 1453. One Greek historian has it that the Sultan Mehmed personally freed them and gave them a choice of a place of refuge in which to settle. Later, however, when Notaras refused to hand over his youngest son Isaac to the Sultan's pleasure, the whole family was executed. Another account related that the wife of Notaras committed suicide rather than face the shame of being taken by the Sultan; and that her sons were killed before her husband's eyes, save for the youngest, Isaac, after whom the Sultan had lusted. He was carried off as a prisoner to Adrianople, though before long he contrived to escape and joined his sister Anna in Italy.[4] Anna's father lived and died as a hero and she never forgot it. A contemporary wrote a funeral oration for him; and Greeks to this day revere Loukas Notaras as the first of their 'national martyrs'.[5]

---

[2] Doukas *Istoria Turco-Bizantină*, ed. V. Grecu (Bucharest, 1958), p. 329.

[3] D. M. Nicol, *The Byzantine Family of Kantakouzenos (Cantacuzenus)* (Washington, D. C., 1968), nos. 68, 69.

[4] The various accounts of the death of Loukas Notaras and his wife and family are summarised in Nicol, *Byzantine Family of Kantakouzenos*, p. 181 n. 17, and in A. Pertusi, *La caduta di Costantinopoli*, 1: *Le testimonianze dei contemporanei* (Verona, 1976), pp. 406–7.

[5] Moschos, John, ed. E. Legrand, Ἰωάννου τοῦ Μόσχου Λόγος ᾿επιτάφιος ᾿επὶ τοῦ Λ. Νοταρᾶ, *DIEE*, II (1885–6), 413–24 (reprinted in Koutibas (see n. 1 above), pp. 39–47); A. E. Vakalopoulos, 'Die Frage der Glaubwürdigkeit der "Leichenrede auf

Anna had been spared the horrors of the sack of Constantinople and of the murder of her parents and siblings. Some years before 1453, when the end of the Byzantine world seemed to be nigh, her father had sent her to the peace and safety of Rome along with her sisters Theodora and Euphrosyne. She went not as a penniless refugee but 'with an ample fortune', and no doubt she could draw on her father's bank accounts in Italy.[6] That he had friends and contacts there is certain. He may well have committed his daughter to the care and protection of Cardinal Bessarion who is known to have been living in Rome between 1440 and 1449. Bessarion, formerly Orthodox Bishop of Nicaea, had been such an eloquent and persuasive advocate of the union between the Greek and Latin churches proclaimed at Florence in 1439 that the Pope had made him a cardinal. In 1463 he was appointed as titular Latin Patriarch of Constantinople. Bessarion regarded himself as protector of all the Greeks in Italy; and he did what he could to help and comfort those who came there as refugees from the Byzantine world before and after 1453. Thomas Palaiologos, brother of the last Byzantine Emperor, who fled from the Peloponnese in 1460, did well out of Bessarion's intercession with Pope Pius II. He had brought with him from Patras the head of the Apostle Andrew and in 1462 Cardinal Bessarion presented it to the Pope. Thomas was rewarded with honours and a pension from the Curia. After his death in 1465 his sons Andrew and Manuel were cared for by Bessarion who looked after them as lawful heirs to the Byzantine throne pending the day when Constantinople would be liberated. That day never came and the two heirs-apparent proved to be a great disappointment to their benefactor Bessarion.[7]

It would be nice to think that Anna Notaras might have been present at the ceremony of the presentation of St Andrew's head to the Pope in Rome in 1462. Pius II left his own account of this great occasion.[8] But his guest list has not survived; and indeed there is no record of Anna and her life in Rome for some years. She had her father's fortune to live on and she never received a pension from the Pope as did some of her distant relatives. She would probably not have accepted such charity, for she could never see eye to eye with the church of Rome. She clung

---

L. Notaras" von Johannes Moschos (15. JH)', *BZ*, LII (1959), 13–21; K. I. Kotsonis, Λουκᾶς ὁ Νοταρᾶς ὁ πρῶτος ἐθνομάρτυς, Ἀκτῖνες, 189 (June 1953), 1–24.

[6] *Ekthesis Chronike*, ed. Sp. P. Lambros, *Ecthesis Chronica and Chronicon Athenarum* (London, 1902), p. 17.

[7] On Thomas Palaiologos, see D. M. Nicol, *The Immortal Emperor. The life and legend of Constantine Palaiologos, last Emperor of the Romans* (Cambridge, 1992), pp. 115–16.

[8] *Commentaries of Pius II*, trans. Florence A. Gragg, ed. Leona Gabel (London, 1960), pp. 241–59.

to her ancestral Orthodox Christianity with a tenacity that embarrassed her Italian hosts. Much as she may have admired the humanity, generosity and scholarship of Cardinal Bessarion, she could never follow him along the road to Rome. Anna was one of the forerunners of the Greek diaspora from Byzantium who felt that their Orthodox faith was vital to their sense of identity and solidarity in an alien world. Bessarion, being himself a Greek, could understand their feelings. He saw it as his duty to bridge the gap between Christians of the Greek east and the Latin west. He could appreciate that Orthodox Christians who had lost their spiritual as well as their material roots were not impressed by his title of Latin Patriarch of Constantinople. Their hero was the monk Gennadios who had spurned the union of Florence and become the first Greek Patriarch of Constantinople after the Turkish conquest. He and his successors may have been the creations or still worse in the pay of the Ottoman Sultans. But they had never doubted the truth of their faith, never compromised it for the sake of supping with the Pope and his cardinals. To the Greeks of the diaspora in western Europe their own Patriarchs of Constantinople were symbols of a continuity of tradition that had been shattered but could be kept alive in the wilderness of exile until such time as the great City and the Great Church were restored to them. Anna Notaras must have learnt to speak Italian but she stubbornly refused to learn the Latin of the Roman Mass.

Cardinal Bessarion died in 1472. The year before his death, and with his encouragement, Anna conceived a plan for setting up a Greek colony on Italian soil. By then her young brother Isaac, the only survivor of the Turkish massacre of her family, had escaped and joined his sister in Rome. He must have been in his early thirties. He was evidently party to her plan. The land on which the colony was to be established belonged to the Commune of Siena. It had once been the estate of a great family in the Maremma, centred around the castle of Montauto which had fallen into ruin. In May 1472 Isaac went to Siena with a request that he be enrolled as a citizen; and in July Anna sent a delegation to Siena to put her proposition to its government. Her ambassadors were Frankoulis Servopoulos, a noble from Constantinople, and John Plousiadenos, a priest from Crete. They were well received and a draft contract was drawn up between Anna and her brother on the one hand and the Commune of Siena on the other. It was agreed that the castle of Montauto in the Maremma should be made over to Anna to be the centre of a community of one hundred Greek families. They would be self-governing and live according to the laws of their past emperors and their own customs as friends and allies of Siena, always ready to come to its aid in emergencies. Anna pledged that she and her successors would never transfer their castle and its estates to any Italian ruler. It seems probable that John Plousiadenos, who was a protégé of Cardinal Bessarion, was intended to be the spiritual leader of the Greek colony; and he was much involved in the long negotiations that followed. Anna's proposal was accepted in principle by the Sienese on 21 July 1472. They may not have been averse to making over a derelict property in the Maremma, a marshy, unproductive and unhealthy strip of land. The draft agreement was reviewed in April 1474 and again, after a letter from Anna in June, on 15 July of the same year. She and her emissaries were made citizens of Siena. But there, for reasons unknown, the matter ended. No Greek colony was founded in Tuscany. Cardinal Bessarion, who had given his blessing to the project, was dead; and Anna moved house to Venice.[9]

A common misconception about Anna's private life derives from her correspondence with the authorities in Siena. In their deliberations of 21 July 1472 they saw fit to describe her as having once been betrothed to the Emperor of the Romans and of Constantinople ('olim sponsae Imperatoris Romanie grecorum et Constantinopolis et filie olim illustris principis domine Luce magni ducis Romanie'). She is similarly described in the Sienese document of July 1474. She herself, however, never claimed such a distinction, being proudly content to be known as the daughter of the Grand Duke Loukas Notaras. Reputable historians of the nineteenth century and later, however, have seized upon this mite of information to declare that Anna Notaras was once betrothed to or even the wife of the last Byzantine Emperor Constantine Palaiologos. Constantine was married twice. Each of his wives died tragically young. He never married a third time, although elaborate schemes were afoot almost to the moment of his death in 1453. They are described in detail by his counsellor and friend, the historian George Sphrantzes. Had there been any question of his marrying the daughter of Loukas Notaras, Sphrantzes would surely have recorded it. Nowhere does he mention Anna by name. Indeed only one of the last Byzantine historians records

---

[9] Anna's dealings with Siena are described and documented by G. Cecchini, 'Anna Notara Paleologa. Una principessa greca in Italia e la politica senese di ripopolamento della Maremma', *Bulletino Senese di Storia Patria*, n.s., IX (1930), 1–41. See also C. N. Sathas, *Documents inédits relatifs á l'histoire de la Grèce au moyen âge*, IX (Paris, 1890), pp. viii–ix, xxxiv–xxxviii. Anna's letter to Siena of 15 June 1474 is printed in full in E. Legrand, ed., *Cent-dix lettres grecques de François Filelfe* (Paris, 1892), p. 540. D. J. Geanakoplos, *Greek Scholars in Venice* (Cambridge, Mass., 1962), p. 62; M. I. Manoussakas, 'Recherches sur la Vie de Jean Plousiadénos (Joseph de Méthone) (1429?–1500)', *REB*, XVII (1959), 41–3. Some sources call Anna's brother Jacob and not Isaac.

that Loukas Notaras had any daughters at all. The misconception must be attributed to the Sienese government, who had probably been misled by the rumours, persistent in Italy at the time, that the last Emperor Constantine left a widow. The evidence that he died unmarried and childless is overwhelming. The evidence that he was ever betrothed to Anna Notaras, such as it is, is mistaken.[10] She liked to describe herself as 'daughter of the late and celebrated Grand Duke Loukas Notaras', as she did in her Will. Sometimes she called herself Anna Palaiologina, a surname which she inherited from her mother. Once she is given the title of 'Hermeneutinam', presumably recalling the official court appellation of [Di]ermeneutes or Interpreter which her father and grandfather had once held.[11] But never does she recall her alleged betrothal to the last Emperor. The only notice of her death specifically records that she died unmarried and a virgin.[12]

She had settled in Venice by 1475. There she seems to have lived with her niece Eudokia Cantacuzene who was already married and had been in Venice for some years. Anna was by then of an age when she might have followed the fashion of ladies of her class by becoming a nun. But she stubbornly refused to go over to the Roman church; and in Venice there was no Orthodox convent for her to enter. Indeed there was no Orthodox church where she and her niece and the growing number of Greek-speaking refugees and immigrants could worship in their own way and language. Of this fact Anna frequently complained to the Venetian authorities. The Venetian attitude towards the Orthodox community in their city was no doubt legally proper but none too tolerant in religious affairs. In the days before the Turkish conquest they had been used to having churches of their own Latin rite in Constantinople. They saw no reason why they should extend similar privileges to foreign refugees who in other respects enjoyed the hospitality of their own city. The Greeks in their view had always been in error and in schism from the true church. It was safer to forbid them from practising and perhaps propagating their heresy by allowing them to worship in their own rite

---

[10] See especially Sp. P. Lambros, Ὁ Κωνσταντῖνος Παλαιολόγος ὡς σύζυγος ἐν τῇ ἱστορίᾳ καὶ τοῖς θρύλοις, NE, IV (1907), 454–8. Anna's betrothal to Constantine Palaiologos is attested in the Sienese documents ed. Cecchini (n. 9 above), nos. 2, 12, 13, pp. 27, 34–41. In documents nos. 6 and 10, p. 33, she signs herself simply as 'Anna Paleologina filia quondam illustris magni ducis Romeorum'. It is accepted as a fact by S. Runciman, 'The marriages of the sons of the Emperor Manuel II', Rivista di Studi Bizantini e Slavi, I (= Miscellanea Agostino Pertusi: Bologna, 1981), 273–82, especially 281. Doukas, ed. Grecu, p. 371, is alone in mentioning the 'daughters' of Loukas Notaras.

[11] Sathas, Documents, IX, p. xxxviii (18 June 1475). See Lambros, NE, IV (1907), 463.

[12] See below. p. 107.

on Venetian territory. In 1412 their Council of Ten asked the Inquisitor of the Holy Office to forbid a Greek priest from celebrating the Orthodox Liturgy in the church of S. Giovanni in Bragora. For a time he was expelled from Venice. In 1415 another Greek priest known to have been ministering to a large congregation in Venice was ordered to desist on pain of being banned from the city for five years. In 1429 two other Greek priests accused of celebrating the Liturgy in private houses were given the same warning.[13]

The much publicised Union of the Greek and Latin Churches promulgated at the Council of Florence in 1439 might have inspired a greater tolerance on both sides. But many of the Greeks in Venice, Anna Notaras among them, saw the union as a betrayal of their own faith; and they were not content with the smug Venetian retort that, now that Christendom was reunited, they could freely frequent the many existing churches in the city. It was a fact, however, as Anna herself complained, that they could not understand the Latin of the Roman Mass. A grudging compromise on the part of the Venetian authorities allowed the Greeks the right to worship in their own language in the side chapel of the church of San Biagio in the district of Castello, provided that their priest subscribed to the Roman form of the Creed and that he did not officiate anywhere else, on pain of a fine. But even there they encountered obstruction. In 1445 a Greek priest who ministered at San Biagio reported his difficulties to Pope Eugenius IV and the Pope wrote to the Bishop of Castello urging him to see that greater tolerance was observed towards the Greeks in Venice, which he knew to be a great number.[14]

After the fall of Constantinople in 1453 the great number became a flood. In June 1456, driven by force majeure more than by generosity, the Venetian Senate voted that Greeks in their city could be allowed to buy a plot of land on which to build a church of their own. This concession was arranged by the eminent refugee Isidore, formerly Orthodox Bishop of Kiev, who had escaped from Constantinople and reached Venice in November 1453. Isidore, like Bessarion, had been so staunch a

---

[13] V. Lamansky, *Secrets d'état de Venise. Documents extraits notices et études servant à éclaircir les rapports de la Seigneurie avec les Grecs et les Slaves et la Porte Ottomane à la fin du XVe et au XVIe siècle* (St Petersburg, 1884), pp. 043, 044; G. Fedalto, *Ricerche storiche sulla posizione giuridiche ed ecclesiastica dei Greci a Venezia nei secoli XV e XVI* (Florence, 1967), pp. 20–22.

[14] Fedalto, *Ricerche*, Appendix, p. 116, Document no. 1. See in general: G. Veludo (Veloudis), Ἑλλήνων Ὀρθοδόξων ἀποικία ʾεν Βενετίᾳ, 2nd ed. (Venice, 1893); P. Pisani, 'Les chrétiens de rite oriental à Venise et dans les possessions vénitiennes (1438–1471)', *Revue d'histoire et de littérature religieuses*, 1 (1896), 201–24.

supporter of the Union of Florence that the Pope had made him a cardinal and appointed him Latin Patriarch of Constantinople in January 1452. It was Cardinal Isidore who persuaded Pope Callixtus III (1455–8) that the growing Greek community in Venice needed a church of their own where they could worship in their own language. He had the backing of the newly created Patriarch of Venice, Maffeo Contarini (1456–60) who, though inclined to distrust the Greeks as unrepentant schismatics, dared not offend the Pope. The senators in Venice therefore had the decision imposed upon them by higher authority.[15]

They were, however, in no hurry to implement it. No land was purchased by the Greeks and no Greek church was built. The resident Greeks had to make do with the unsatisfactory arrangements for their Orthodox worship in the church of San Biagio; and even there the priests in charge had to submit to examination by the Patriarch of Venice on the correctness of their Catholic faith. Their champion Cardinal Isidore died in 1463; and there matters rested for some years. Anna's persistence, however, won an exceptional privilege for herself and her niece Eudokia. On 18 June 1475 the Council of Ten granted them permission to construct an oratory in their own house for the celebration of the Orthodox Liturgy in their own language. It was a privilege grudgingly granted and at first only on condition that it was confined to Anna's household and was not to be shared with any other Greeks. When, four years later, it was proposed that the privilege be extended to all Greeks living in Venice, one of the Venetian councillors objected that this was a sure way of imperilling the Catholic faith by the infection of 'the Greek schism'. He was overruled. But for unknown reasons the new Venetian liberality remained no more than a promise. Anna had to content herself with the privileges which had been accorded to her personally; and they were extended by governmental decrees in September 1480 and in May 1489.[16] The Greek clergy in Venice, however, grew increasingly impatient with the restrictions imposed upon them. One of them, a priest called Andrew of Modon, caused a great stir in 1498 by appealing directly to the Pope in the name of all the Greek community, lay and clerical. He suggested that they should all come under the jurisdiction not of the Patriarch of Venice but of the Latin Patriarch of Constantinople, the successor of Cardinals Bessarion and Isidore, who would in future appoint all their priests.

---

[15] M. I. Manoussakas, Ἡ πρώτη ἄδεια (1456) τῆς Βενετικῆς γερουσίας γιὰ τὸν ναὸν τῶν Ἑλλήνων τῆς Βενετίας καὶ ὁ καρδινάλιος Ἰσίδωρος, *Thesaurismata*, I (1962), 109–18.

[16] Lamansky, *Secrets d'état de Venise* pp. 053, 057–8; Sathas, *Documents*, IX, pp. x, xxxviii–xl; Fedalto, *Ricerche*, pp. 40–2 and Appendix, p. 124, Document no. XI.

This was too much for the Venetian authorities. The Council of Ten at once got in touch with the Curia, observing that such a move would be an insult to the authority of the Patriarch of Venice and an offence against the constitution of Venice. It would create confusion in the church and the Pope should be dissuaded from considering it. The Greeks must be reminded that they were in Venice only under sufferance and that they were still suspected of doctrinal errors.[17]

In her latter years Anna became the acknowledged spokesman and patroness of the Greek community in Venice. The Venetians respected her for her wealth, her aristocratic lineage and her influence. Her father had known Cardinal Isidore in Constantinople. Her niece Eudokia married a Greek soldier who rose to high rank in the service of Venice. He was one of a rapidly growing number. In 1479 it was reckoned that there were between 4000 and 5000 Greek residents in Venice. They were not idle scroungers. They served the interests of their hosts in a number of ways. As the Turks advanced further and further west into the remaining Venetian colonies in Greece and the eastern Mediterranean, the Venetian government recruited companies of light-armed cavalrymen from among the Greeks who were eager to fight against the common enemy. They were known as the *stradioti* from the Greek word for soldier; and many of the sons and grandsons of the first refugees from Byzantium enlisted in their ranks to fight for Venice. Anna's niece Eudokia Cantacuzene had married one of the more distinguished of the *stradioti* before 1460. He was Matthew Spandounes or Spandugnino, whose exploits earned him the title of Count and Knight of the Holy Roman Empire. One of her sons was Theodore Spandounes who in 1538 wrote one of the earliest accounts of the origins of the Ottoman Empire.[18] Eudokia's husband as well as her aunt Anna Notaras clearly had influence in high places. In 1494 the Greeks in Venice were permitted to found a Brotherhood of the Greek race, a philanthropic and religious society with its own officers and committee to represent the interests of the Greek community. It was the first formal recognition by Venice of the legal status of the Greek colony. But it was not until 1539 that they were authorised to begin building their own church of San Giorgio dei Greci which still stands in the centre of Venice on the Rio dei Greci. Anna was by then long dead. But

---

[17] Lamansky, *Secrets d'état de Venise*, p. 053.
[18] Nicol, *Byzantine Family of Kantakouzenos*, pp. xv–xvii, 230–33.

she had not lived in vain in pressing the legal and spiritual rights of her compatriots in a foreign land.[19]

One of the greatest contributions of the Greeks in Venice in the fifteenth century was their dissemination of Greek scholarship, philosophy and literature. Many of them fled from Byzantium bringing manuscripts of ancient Greek works. They knew that there was a ready market for such treasures, particularly in Florence where the study of ancient Greek had become fashionable. Cardinal Bessarion had shown the way before he died by giving his large library of Greek and Latin manuscripts to the Republic of Venice where it formed the nucleus of the great library of St Mark. Anna Notaras no doubt encouraged any move to make Greek more widely known in Italy, although the evidence for her own scholarly tastes is slender. Given her passion for the Orthodox faith she may well have felt, as many Byzantines had felt before her, that the legacy of pagan Greek philosophy and literature could be dangerous for Christian readers. Evidently she kept a library of her own, for in 1470 she acquired a twelfth-century manuscript of a Catena of Job written by one John Tarsites for Leon Nikerites, once Grand Duke of Cyprus. Maybe she was attracted by the fact that the original owner of the manuscript had held the same title as her father. The record of her having acquired it, on 1 March 1470, is written in a later hand at the end of the manuscript and proudly describes her as Anna, daughter of Loukas Notaras, Grand Duke of Constantinople.[20]

The invention of typography had an electrifying effect on the dissemination of Greek learning and literature in Renaissance Italy. Greek type faces were cut and Greek printing presses were assembled. The enterprising Aldus Manutius was quick to see that Venice had a ready supply of marketable material to be printed in Greek. It had scholars from Byzantium who could edit the material for the press. It had a crowd of literate Greeks who could act as compositors and typesetters. Above all it had the manuscripts which many of them had brought with them. But Aldus was not the first in the field. Some of the Greeks

[19] D. J. Geanakoplos, 'The Greco-Byzantine colony in Venice and its significance in the Renaissance', in *Byzantine East and Latin West* (Oxford, 1966), pp. 116–21; Geanakoplos, *Greek Scholars in Venice*, pp. 61–9; D. M. Nicol, *Byzantium and Venice. A study in diplomatic and cultural relations* (Cambridge, 1988), pp. 415–17.

[20] Cod. Vat. gr. 1231. Lambros, *NE*, IV (1907), 459–60; V (1908), 485–6. P. Canart and V. Peri, *Sussidi Bibliografici per i manoscritti greci della Biblioteca Vaticana* (Studi e Testi 261: Vatican City, 1970), pp. 559–60; J. Darrouzès, 'Autres manuscrits originaires de Chypre', *REB*, xv (1957), 156, no. 117; M. Vogel and V. Gardthausen, *Die griechischen Schreiber des Mittelalters und der Renaissance* (Leipzig, 1909), p. 201.

too had seen that the new technology presented a new opportunity for spreading interest in their own tradition and inheritance. One of the first was a talented Cretan called Zacharias Kalliergis who had settled in Venice at an early age. Kalliergis was keenly interested in Greek calligraphy and he pioneered the setting up in Venice of a press devoted exclusively to printing works in Greek. The first of his splendid productions, the Etymologicum Magnum, was published in Venice on 8 July 1499. It had taken him six years to perfect and produce. It remains one of the most beautiful examples of Greek typography, printed in black and red. It is equipped with some dedicatory verses and a preface by Mark Musurus, friend and collaborator of Aldus Manutius; and on its final pages it carries an inscription recording that the cost of the production was defrayed 'by the noble and esteemed Cretan Nicholas Vlastos, on the recommendation of the most distinguished and most modest lady Anna, daughter of ... Loukas Notaras, once Grand Duke of Constantinople'. On its last pages, printed in red and side by side on facing folios, are the printers' emblems of Zacharias Kalliergis, the Byzantine double-headed eagle, and his business partner Nicholas Vlastos.[21]

There could be no more exquisite and sumptuous advertisement of Anna's patronage of Greek scholarship. As its dedication declares, it was printed 'by the labour and skill of Zacharias Kalliergis the Cretan, for the benefit of learned men and those set on [the study of] Hellenic literature'. There can be little doubt that Anna's modesty restrained her from revealing her own contribution to the project. She probably secured the permission and the imprimatur of the Venetian Senate. Some of her private wealth surely went into the production of this masterpiece of printing. It has even been suggested that some of the decorations of the page headings and capital letters in the text were based on embroideries which Anna and her niece Eudokia had worked.[22] Nicholas Vlastos, who gets the credit for financing the publication, is known to have been Anna's factor or manager of her estate. He is also known to have copied manuscripts with his own hand.[23] He paid the cost of the second publication of Kalliergis, the 1499 printed edition of the Commentaries of Simplicius on Aristotle's Categories. Anna is not mentioned in the credits for this edition. Perhaps in her pious way she felt that she could give her blessing to a pure work of

---

[21] On Nicholas Vlastos, see C. Kerofilas, *Une famille patricienne Crétoise. Les Vlasto* (New York, 1932), pp. 79–108; Geanakoplos, *Greek Scholars in Venice*, pp. 204–8.

[22] Sathas, *Documents*, IX, p. xi.

[23] Vogel and Gardthausen, *Die griechischen Schreiber*, p. 346.

reference like the Etymologicum Magnum. Aristotle was another matter.[24]

At the time when Kalliergis was just embarking on his first great publication, in 1493, Anna made her Will. A copy of it exists in the Archivo di Stato in Venice. The text is said to be signed by Anna in her own hand. This is hard to believe, for it is written in a form of Greek so illiterate and demotic that it would not have been countenanced by one who prized the style of the Etymologicum Magnum. It can hardly be the original manuscript of her Will. It was written and witnessed by her father confessor the priest Ioannes Kapnisis, a Greek name which, if correctly transcribed, is not otherwise attested; and it is dated 24 March 1493. Anna identifies herself as the daughter of the most illustrious and renowned Loukas Notaras, Grand Duke of Constantinople. She expresses her thanks to the Procurator of Venice, Nicolo Mocenigo; to the President of the Council of Ten, Giovanni Pisani; to her sister Theodora; and above all to Nicholas Vlastos, her factor and administrator of her estate. She recalls how Vlastos had been imprisoned and subjected to torture for three years, unjustly in her view, perhaps because of his involvement in the anti-Venetian rebellion of Crete led by his relative Siphis Vlastos in the 1450s and 1460s.[25] It is her wish that they will pray for her according to the rite of 'Romaic' (Orthodox) Christians. True to her lifelong dream, she sets aside 500 ducats from her estate for the construction of a Romaic church in Venice so that always and in perpetuity the Orthodox may pray for her soul and the souls of her parents and family. Further, she wishes to pay for the ransom and liberation from the Turks of a Christian prisoner, for this had been the wish of her sister Euphrosyne just before she died. The residue of her estate was to be spent partly on erecting a monument to herself and all her family; and to her uncle Demetrios Asen she bequeathed the sum of 6 ducats a year for the rest of his life. The only unpleasant note in Anna's Will is her rude reference to her sister-in-law Zampeta or Elizabeth, presumably the wife of her brother Isaac. She instructs her executors to have nothing to do with this member of the family or anyone repre-

---

[24] On Zacharias Kalliergis, see Geanakoplos, Greek Scholars in Venice, pp. 201–22. On his edition of the Etymologicum magnum, see E. Legrand, Bibliographie hellénique, ou description raisonnée des ouvrages en grec publiés par des Grecs au XVe et XVI e siècle, 1 (Paris, 1885), pp. 55–62; H. Brown, The Venetian Printing Press 1469–1800 (London, 1891; repr. Amsterdam, 1969), pp. 43–4; R. Proctor, The Printing of Greek in the Fifteenth Century (Oxford, 1900), pp. 118–19; M. Manoussakas and K. Staikos, ed., The Publishing Activity of the Greeks during the Italian Renaissance (Benaki Museum: Athens, 1987), pp. 130–7.

[25] A. E. Vakalopoulos, Ἱστορία τοῦ Νεοελληνισμοῦ, 1, 2nd ed. (Thessaloniki, 1974), pp. 171–2.

senting her, since she has squandered all of Isaac's fortune.[26] The Venetian notary who filed Anna's Will, Troylo Manfredi, noted on its cover that she was ignorant of Latin, thus confirming the statement that she herself had made in May 1487.[27]

From the text of this interesting document it emerges that Anna's sister Euphrosyne and her brother Isaac were dead by 1493, though her sister Theodora was still alive. Her uncle Demetrios Asen, to whom she left an annuity, must have been very elderly. He might have been the Demetrios Asen whom the humanist Francesco Filelfo knew in Italy. Her niece Eudokia Cantacuzene does not figure in the Will, though she is known to have been still alive in 1488. Eudokia's gallant husband Matthew Spandounes, the Count of the Holy Roman Empire, died before 1511.[28] Anna herself died in Venice on 8 July 1507 at an advanced age. The fact is tersely recorded in a note of that date in the Diaries of Marino Sanuto: 'a Greek lady who had lived in this country died at San Giuliano. She was the daughter of ... who was a man of high estate in Constantinople in the time of the Emperor Paleologo. She was more than a hundred years old and she died a virgin. She was rich.'[29] She can hardly have been quite as old as Sanuto reports. But she had had a long and busy life. Thirty more years were to pass before her dream of founding an Orthodox church in Venice was realised. It is to be hoped that she had a Greek priest to minister to her on her deathbed and to bury her in 1507. She would never have rested in a Roman grave.

She makes no mention in her Will of the magnificent icons which she presented to the Greek community in Venice. The archives of the Greek Brotherhood, however, record that three of the icons now in the church of San Giorgio dei Greci or the Hellenic Institute in Venice were the gift of the 'Grand Duchess Anna Notaras who had brought them with her from Constantinople' before 1453. They are Constantinopolitan in style and date from the late fourteenth century. One is a large painting showing Christ in glory surrounded by the symbols of the Evangelists and framed on either side by figures of the twelve Apostles.[30] The second, in the iconostasis of the church, is similar in style, showing Christ Pantokrator and in the margins miniatures of

[26] K. C. Mertzios, Ἡ Διαθήκη τῆς Ἄννας Παλαιολογίνας Νοταρᾶ, *Athena*, LIII (1949), 17–21. Reprinted in Koutibas (see n. 1 above), pp. 59–62.

[27] Sathas, *Documents*, IX, p. xxxix.

[28] I. Božilov, *Familijata na Asenevci (1186–1460). Genealogija i Prosopografija* (Sofia, 1985), no. 76, pp. 390–1; Nicol, *Byzantine Family of Kantakouzenos*, no. 102.

[29] Sanuto, *Diarii di Marino Sanuto*, ed. R. Fulin, VII (Venice, 1882), p. 115.

[30] M. Chatzidakis, *Icônes de Saint-Georges des Grecs et de la Collection de l'Institut*, Bibliothèque de l'Institut Hellénique d'Etudes Byzantines et Post-Byzantines de Venise, 1

Mara charitably ministered to the needs of the Christians in her
ourhood but she also made it her business to act as an interme-
on her husband's behalf and she earned much respect at the
ish court for her loyalty to his interests. It was her two brothers,
ory and Stephen, who returned to Serbia in 1435, who looked for
ole.[6] In 1438 the Sultan urged Mara to exercise her influence on her
er to sever his alliance with Hungary and bury the hatchet. It was to
avail. George Branković would not surrender any more of Serbia to
Turks. The ravenous dragon had eaten enough. He took his stand in
newly finished fortress at Smederevo. In the following year the
ltan, no doubt in spite of Mara's pleading and certainly in breach of
s treaty with her father, marched into Serbia. He led his own army.
mederevo was strongly defended by Mara's father and her brother
Gregory, although he was only about fifteen years old. Also among the
defenders was her uncle Thomas Cantacuzene, one of many Greeks
who had entered the service of the Despot of Serbia. The Turkish siege
lasted for three months until, on 18 August 1439, Smederevo had to
surrender. Murad was now truly master of almost all of Serbia.[7]

Mara's father was allowed to stay in Serbia and lick his wounds. His
castle had surrendered because its defenders were hungry. They had
opened their gates to the ravenous dragon. They were therefore spared
the customary plunder and carnage meted out by the Turks to those
who resisted conquest. They had indeed held out for three months; but
the Sultan may have been moved to leniency by the thought that their
leader, George Branković, was his father-in-law. Mara's uncle Thomas
Cantacuzene was also allowed to survive and to fight again another day.
Her brother Gregory, however, was rounded up and taken to join his
brother Stephen who was with their sister at Adrianople. Not long
afterwards both of the young men were accused of secret correspondence with their father in Serbia. They were imprisoned and then
removed to Amaseia in Asia Minor where, for all the entreaties of
Mara, their eyes were put out, on 8 May 1441. One much later account
has it that they were back visiting their sister Mara at Adrianople and

[5] The name and identity of Murad's first wife, the mother of Mehmed II, remains
uncertain. See F. Babinger, *Mehmed the Conqueror and his Time*, transl. R. Mannheim,
ed. W. C. Hickman (Princeton, N.J., 1978), pp. 11–12; S. Runciman, *The Fall of Constantinople 1453* (Cambridge, 1965), p. 55 identifies her as Huma Hatun, a Turkish slave
girl.
[6] On Gregory (Grgur) and Stephen (Stjepan), see Nicol, *Byzantine Family of Kantakouzenos*, nos. 93, 95.
[7] On Thomas Cantacuzene, see Nicol, *Byzantine Family of Kantakouzenos*, no. 70.

sixteen figures, twelve Apostles and four Prophets.[31] The third is an
icon of the Virgin Hodegetria and has been identified with the miraculous icon from Constantinople known as the 'Krypti' or secret. This
identification is certainly wrong, since the original Krypti is known to
have been stolen or lost in 1540.[32] These precious and holy pictures were
some of Anna's personal links with her past. They may have belonged
to her parents or to the Notaras family in Constantinople before she
took them with her to safety in Italy. Perhaps they hung in her private
chapel in Venice before she gave them for safe-keeping to the
Brotherhood which was founded in 1494. After her death they found a
proper home in the church of St George of the Greeks for the foundation of which she had worked so hard.

(Venice, 1962), no. 2, pp. 7–8 and plate 1; VIII (Venice, 1975), plate 2; M I
Manoussakas and A. D. Paliouras, Ὀδηγὸς τοῦ Μουσείου τῶν Εἰκόνων καὶ τοῦ Ναοῦ
τοῦ Ἁγίου Γεωργίου (Venice, 1976), no. 29, p. 33 and plate 9; Maria Christina
Bandera Viani, *Venezia. Museo delle Icone Bizantine e post Bizantine e Chiesa di San
Giorgio dei Greci* (Bologna, 1988) no. 29, pp. 23–4 and plates 29, 29 a–b.
[31] Chatzidakis, *Icônes*, I, no. 1, pp. 4–6 and plate 1; Manoussakas and Paliouras, no. 194,
p. 55 and plate 27; Viani, *Venezia*, no. 194, p. 98 and plate 194.
[32] Chatzidakis, *Icônes*, I, no. 4, pp. 11–13 and plates 3 and 4; VIII, plate 4; Manoussakas
and Paliouras, no. 204, p. 56; Viani, *Venezia*, no. 204, pp. 103–4 and plate 204.

CHAPTER NINE

———— ❦ ————

MARA BRANKOVIĆ OF SERBIA,
SULTANINA
C. 1412–1476

MARA, known to the Greeks as Maria, was one of the most remarkable products of the melting pot of ruling families that banded together for survival in the Balkans during and after the Turkish conquest of the Byzantine Empire in the fifteenth century. Her father was George Branković of Serbia. He was to be glorified with the Byzantine title of Despot in 1429 by the Emperor John VIII. But, like all the remaining Christian princes of eastern Europe from the Emperor downwards, Branković ruled his principality under sufferance of the Ottoman Turks. He played a hazardous game of pretending to be their faithful vassal while at the same time trying to build up a Christian coalition to stem the tide of their victorious advance. In 1427 he made an alliance with his neighbour the King of Hungary. Three years later he built the huge fortress of Smederevo on the Danube near Belgrade. It was to be the last capital of medieval Christian Serbia and its last defence against the Turks.

George Branković was married twice, first to a sister of the Emperor of distant Trebizond, John IV Komnenos, then to Eirene of the family of Cantacuzene. Mara was the daughter of his first wife and since the date of his second marriage is known to have been the year 1414, she must have been born about 1412.[1] Her stepmother Eirene produced three sons and one daughter. Mara as the eldest of his family was a valuable commodity in her father's dealings with the Turks. He could buy their friendship or their peace by agreeing to give her as a bride to their Sultan, Murad II. Precedents had been set for such marriages

[1] The principal Byzantine sources for Mara's career are the historians Doukas, Sphrantzes and Chalkokondyles. There is a great quantity of secondary material, mainly in Serbian, though some in Greek. The main facts of her life with the sources are listed in D. M. Nicol, *The Byzantine Family of Kantakouzenos (Cantacuzenus)* (Washington, D.C., 1968), no. 92, pp. 210–13; *PLP*, VII, no. 17210 (s.v. Μάρω), where she is described as the eldest daughter of the second marriage of George Branković.

between Christian and Muslim rulers. In the [...] circumstances of the fifteenth century Christ[...] sometimes gave way to expediency. The bride [...] say in the matter. According to the Byzantine h[...] the Sultan who made the proposal. He reasone[...] himself a lot of trouble by taking Mara to wife and [...] bring with her most of Serbia as her dowry. Her [...] hand, reasoned that the best way to placate a ravenou[...] it until it becomes drowsy and mellow from over-indu[...] a mutually convenient arrangement. In June 1433 the S[...] one of his viziers, Sarugan Pasha, to Serbia to negoti[...] contract was drawn up and Mara was legally betrothed [...] The extent of her dowry was noted by the vizier as bei[...] part of Serbia' as well as untold sums of gold and silver. O[...] George Branković bought peace from the Turks.[2]

In 1433 Mara was about twenty-one years old. The Sultan [...] was to marry was thirty-six. He already had a wife by Musli[...] we are told, he came to love Mara more deeply for, of the tw[...] more beautiful in mind and in body.[3] The betrothal was binding [...] wedding had to wait for some months until Murad could spa[...] from his incessant military campaigns. Not until the autumn o[...] was he at leisure. His vizier was despatched back to Serbia to [...] Mara and escort her to Murad's palace at Adrianople (Edirne), w[...] was then the capital of the Ottoman dominions in Europe. Her fat[...] perhaps wisely, stayed where he was at Smederevo. But she brou[...] with her her two little brothers, Gregory and Stephen. The weddin[...] was celebrated with great festivities at Adrianople on 4 September 1435[...] It was a Muslim ceremony and therefore unacceptable to the Orthodox church in which Mara had been reared. But she put up with it and, we are assured, remained steadfast in her Christian faith and faithful to her infidel husband, though often keeping an eye open for ways in which she might be of service to her father in Serbia and to the Christian cause in general. She was not a spy but she was a useful agent trusted on both sides.[4]

She was an intelligent woman and quick to learn. She evidently soon mastered the etiquette of life in a harem and treated her husband's first wife with proper tact and respect. She had after all already borne him a son, three years before Mara took his fancy. The boy's name was Mehmed, later to be known as the Conqueror, and he was born in

[2] Doukas, *Historia Turco-Byzantină (1341–1462)*, ed. V. Grecu (Bucharest, 1958), p. 257.
[3] Doukas, ed. Grecu, p. 259.   [4] *Ibid.*, pp. 257–8.

that her husband had them blinded simply out of jealousy of their youthful prowess on the hunting field.[8]

Mara was condemned to live with her Turkish husband for another ten years, fulfilling her duties as Sultanina. Her brothers, condemned to darkness, were sent back to their father in Serbia after he had made a new settlement with the Sultan. The terms had been agreed at Adrianople in 1444 and Mara had a part in arranging them. In the same year Murad annihilated the coalition of western Christian powers that had been sent to dislodge the Turks from Europe, the so-called crusade of Varna. It was the last of the great international crusades against the infidel.[9] A few months later he retired from active duty as Sultan and delegated his authority to his son Mehmed who was hardly thirteen years old. Murad withdrew to Manisa in Asia Minor, taking with him only a few trusted friends and companions. Mara presumably went with him. He had to return to Adrianople from time to time in the next few years and even to lead campaigns as far afield as Albania. He had taken to heavy drinking and it was during one of his bouts on his favourite island in the river near Adrianople that he died of apoplexy on 3 February 1451. He was only forty-seven. He had been a mild and usually moderate man. There is no hint that he ever ill-treated or misused his Christian wife. It was rumoured that their marriage was never consummated. Even the Greek historians of the time praised him for his honesty and justice.[10]

Mara may even have mourned his passing. But once he was gone she longed to return to her own country and her own people. The mother of the new Sultan, Mehmed, had died in 1449. He had known Mara all his life and had come to honour and admire her. Throughout his long and triumphant reign Mehmed II looked upon her as a mother-substitute and often called upon her for advice. It was to Mara's advantage that her marriage to Murad was childless. Had she borne a son he would always have been suspect as a potential rival to the Sultan Mehmed. She must have known or learnt after the event that Mehmed had caused another of Murad's sons to be drowned in his bath, a crime which came to be legalised as the law of fratricide at every future succession to the Ottoman Sultanate.[11]

Mara soon had her wish to be allowed to return to Serbia. Her father

---

[8] Doukas, ed. Grecu, pp. 261–3; Theodore Spandounes (Spandugnino), *De la origine deli Imperatori Ottomani* ..., ed. C. N. Sathas, *Documents inédits relatifs à l'histoire de la Grèce au moyen âge*, IX (Paris, 1890), pp. 152–3. Babinger, *Mehmed*, pp. 16–19.

[9] Babinger, *Mehmed*, pp. 32–42; Nicol, *Last Centuries of Byzantium*, pp. 361–3.

[10] Babinger, *Mehmed*, pp. 60–3.

[11] Babinger, *Mehmed*, pp. 65–6.

George Branković very properly and diplomatically sent envoys from Smederevo to commiserate with Mehmed on the sad death of his father and to seek a renewal of his treaty with Serbia. He also begged that his daughter Mara, the late Sultan's widow, be given leave to return to her parents. The Serbian envoys escorted her home, the richer by gifts and pleasantries.[12] She found that she had become famous. In the Christian world she was known as the *amerissa* or widow of the Emir, or as Sultanina, or even as the *imperatrix* by those who knew little Latin and less Turkish. She had become a precious pawn in the diplomatic manoeuvres of the age. She was not given much time to enjoy being back in the bosom of her family in Serbia. After only a few months a suggestion was made that she might marry the widowed Emperor of Constantinople, Constantine XI Palaiologos. He had been married twice and each of his wives had died tragically young without bearing a child. The future of the Byzantine Empire looked gloomy enough. It might look more promising if there were an heir to its throne. The Emperor's advisers considered a number of ladies as suitable Empresses, a daughter of the King of Georgia and a daughter of the Emperor of Trebizond. When Mara came on the matrimonial market some thought that she would be an ideal choice. The matter was put to her parents. They were delighted at the prospect of their daughter being married to the Emperor and welcomed the idea. For Mara it would have been a unique achievement that would have immortalised her as the lady who married first a Muslim Sultan and then a Christian Emperor. But she was not seeking publicity. She firmly declined to have anything to do with the project. For she had vowed that if God ever released her from the hands of the infidel she would lead a chaste and celibate life for the rest of her days. Nothing would change her mind.[13]

It says much for Mara's maturity and strength of character that she so obstinately refused to obey her father's wishes in this matter. Like many a Byzantine widow before her she might have insured herself against further inroads on her privacy by becoming a nun. She preferred to stay in the secular world, surrounded by her family and relatives. The world would not leave her alone, however. In 1454–5 she successfully fought off another attempt to wish a husband upon her. He was one Jovan

---

[12] Doukas, ed. Grecu, pp. 287–9. Babinger, *Mehmed*, pp. 59, 66.
[13] Sphrantzes, *Chronicon minus*, p. 78–82. D. M. Nicol, *The Immortal Emperor. The life and legend of Constantine Palaiologos, last Emperor of the Romans* (Cambridge, 1992), pp. 43–6.

Jiskra, a Czech captain who had come to fight for her father in Serbia. Again she resisted the proposal.[14]

Her father George Branković died in December 1456, her step-mother Eirene a few months later, in May 1457. Rumour had it that Eirene had been poisoned by her youngest son Lazar, who was determined to make his name as Despot of Serbia by eliminating all other claimants. Mara was justifiably afraid of Lazar and, on the night of Eirene's death, she fled from Smederevo together with her blind brother Gregory and her uncle Thomas. Lazar pursued them and apprehended them. But Mara with Gregory contrived to escape. She threw herself on the mercy and protection of her stepson the Sultan Mehmed II who was by then master of Constantinople. He received her warmly and made arrangements for her well-being. She was aware that the conquest of Serbia was high on the list of Mehmed's future plans and she rightly opted to be on the winning side, leaving her brothers Lazar and Stephen, who had stayed with him, to play at being heroes in the defence of Smederevo against the Sultan's army. Lazar was spared the end of the drama. He died in 1458. Stephen fled to Hungary; and in 1459 the Turks moved in to Smederevo. It was the end of the Despotate of Serbia.[15]

Thereafter Mara lived comfortably under the protection and favour of her stepson, the conquering Sultan Mehmed II. He was glad to have her back and treated her with the honour due to a mother figure. He settled her on an estate of her own at Ježevo, formerly called Daphni, in eastern Macedonia between Serres and Mount Athos. Her brother Gregory left her to become a monk in the Serbian monastery of Chilandari on the Holy Mountain and died in October 1459. In March of that year the Sultan gave proof of his special care and regard for Mara by granting her full and inalienable possession of the monastery of St Sophia in Thessalonica and all its revenues.[16] It was an extraordinary gesture of trust and friendship. Later Sultans were not so tolerant nor so generous to their Christian subjects. Some fifty years after Mara's death

[14] L. von Thalloczy, *Studien zur Geschichte Bosniens und Serbiens im Mittelalter* (Munich and Leipzig, 1914), p. 124. The documentary source for Jovan Jiskra calls him 'Pan Isera'. Nicol, *Byzantine Family of Kantakouzenos*, p. 211 n. 3; M. Spremić, 'Dva podatka Mari Branković', *Istorijski Glasnik*, 1–2 (Belgrade, 1977), 71–80; *PLP*, VII, no. 17210, p. 140.

[15] Kritoboulos of Imbros, ed. V. Grecu (Bucharest, 1963), pp. 205–9. Babinger, *Mehmed*, pp. 162–4; Nicol, *Byzantine Family of Kantakouzenos*, pp. 212, 215, 222.

[16] The Sultan's *firman* was edited by F. Babinger, 'Ein Freibrief Mehmeds II, des Eroberers, für das Kloster Hagia Sophia zu Saloniki, Eigentum des Sultanin Mara (1459)', *BZ*, XLIV (1951), 11–20; Babinger, *Mehmed*, pp. 163–4.

the church of St Sophia was to be converted into a mosque. In the document (*firman*) recording Mehmed's deed of gift he describes Mara as 'my mother Despina Hatun' and 'the *amerissa*, mistress of the Christian noblewomen'. She was by no means a neglected and destitute refugee. She held court at Ježevo surrounded by exiled Serbian nobles and monks; for she remained, as Doukas observed, 'a most Christian lady' and was a great comfort to other Christians less fortunate than herself under Turkish rule.[17] Ambassadors from western Europe, especially from Venice, on their way to negotiate with the Sultan or his minions at the Porte, would sometimes make detours to seek the advice of the great man's stepmother. They called her the 'marengo del gran Turco', or 'madregna del Imperador'.

In 1469 she was joined at Ježevo by her elder sister Catherine who bore the name of Cantacuzene and had married the noble and wealthy Ulrich II, Count of Cilly. Her fortunes had changed after he was assassinated in 1456 and she led a chequered if exciting life until Mara obtained the Sultan's permission to invite her to stay at Ježevo.[18] The two ladies then operated a kind of unofficial foreign office from eastern Macedonia. They maintained diplomatic relations with and received ambassadors from Ragusa (Dubrovnik), where Catherine had property interests, from Venice and from Constantinople. In the war between Venetians and Turks from 1463 to 1479 they played an important role as intermediaries and were employed by both sides as diplomatic agents. In 1471 Mara personally accompanied a Venetian ambassador to the Porte for negotiations with the Sultan. They knew that she had a way with him. Two years earlier she and her sister had tried to interest the Republic of Venice in purchasing a number of Christian relics which were then in Turkish hands, among them the tunic of Christ. The Venetians expressed great interest, for it would be a work of Christian charity, if the asking price was reasonable. They knew their business in these affairs. They had once put a price on the Crown of Thorns. Perhaps they found the price too high, for nothing came of the deal.[19]

Among the guests who stayed at Ježevo were Mara's niece Maria and the young Theodore Spandounes, whose father Matthew was related by marriage to Anna Notaras, patroness of the Greek community in Venice. Mara and Catherine were Theodore's great-aunts, and it was probably while staying with them that he acquired his knowledge of the history and civilisation of the Ottoman Turks which he later com-

---

[17] Doukas, ed. Grecu, p. 287.
[18] On Catherine Cantacuzene, see Nicol, *Byzantine Family of Kantakouzenos*, no. 94.
[19] Babinger, *Mehmed*, pp. 276, 289, 297, 341; *PLP*, VII, p. 131.

mitted to writing and to print.[20] The ramifications and family connexions of Mara and her sister, through the houses of Branković and Cantacuzene, encompassed all of what had once been the Byzantine Empire, eastern Europe and Venice. Like Anna Notaras, Mara, although not overtly hostile to the Turks, saw it as part of her duty to care for and support the Orthodox Christians living in her stepson's dominions. She was a conscientious protectress of the Serbian monastery of Chilandari on Mount Athos in which her brother Gregory had died, and also of the monastery of St Paul, which her father George Branković had endowed. In 1479 she enriched both institutions with annual incomes from her own purse.[21]

Mara's influence in high places extended to the appointment of leaders of the church. In her time the Patriarch of Constantinople was still the spiritual head of the universal Orthodox church. But the Sultan also held him responsible for the behaviour of all Christians living under Turkish rule. The first Patriarch of Constantinople to be faced with these responsibilities after the conquest of the city in 1453 was Gennadios Scholarios. He was appointed and installed by the Sultan Mehmed. A precedent had been set. It soon became the rule that future and aspiring Patriarchs would seek the Sultan's favour for their candidature by bribery, agreeing to pay to the Ottoman treasury an annual sum of money and a present to the Sultan's officials. Early in 1465 one Mark Xylokarabes ascended the patriarchal throne. His rival, Symeon of Trebizond, raised the sum of 2000 gold coins and presented it to the Sultan who obligingly ordered him to be appointed as Patriarch in place of Mark. When Mara heard of this simony she made straight for the Sultan's court, taking with her 2000 gold coins of her own, and persuaded Mehmed to dismiss both Mark and Symeon and replace them by her own candidate. He was a monk called Dionysios, Bishop of Philippopolis, who had acted as spiritual adviser to Mara. The Sultan was glad of the money but rather tired of the whole business and he gave her leave to end it all by saying simply: 'Thank you, my mother, do what you please.' Dionysios was perhaps too saintly a man to stay as Patriarch in such circumstances. His rivals soon had him removed and, again thanks to Mara's intervention, he was allowed to retire to the peace of his monastery at Kosinitza, not far from Mara's residence.[22]

[20] On Anna Notaras and Theodore Spandounes, see Nicol, *Byzantine Family of Kantakouzenos*, pp. xv–xviii and 230–3, and above pp. 104–5.

[21] Nicol, *Byzantine Family of Kantakouzenos*, p. 213.

[22] Nicol, *Byzantine Family of Kantakouzenos*, p. 212; S. Runciman, *The Great Church in Captivity* (Cambridge, 1968), pp. 193–4.

Mara continued, none the less, to consider it her Christian duty to play a leading role in the affairs of the Orthodox church. Symeon bought his way back into the patriarchate, but three years later he was ousted by another of Mara's protégés, a Serbian monk called Raphael, who promised another 2000 gold coins to the Sultan and 500 to the courtiers. Raphael was not a success as Patriarch. He had trouble raising the money for his appointment. The Greeks disliked him as a foreigner and found reasons for getting him deposed. He was reduced to wandering the streets of Constantinople as a beggar and died in prison. Once again Mara stepped in to propose a successor who was duly invested as Patriarch by her stepson.[23]

In the latter part of her life, thanks to the esteem in which the Sultan Mehmed held her, Mara was able to keep a balance between Christians and Turks. It may have been thought that she was something of a busybody in ecclesiastical affairs; and the Sultan would surely have stepped in if she had shown any sign of seeking the support of the church of Rome. For it was in his interest to keep the Christians divided. None the less, her influence was known and felt in Venice and in Constantinople as well as in the half-way house of Ragusa, where she kept a family bank account and agents to work for her. Her estates in Macedonia were limited in extent. But with the continuing favour of the Sultan Mehmed and indeed of his successor Bayezid II, she was in some sense a forerunner of the Phanariote princes of the eighteenth century who ruled the principalities of Wallachia and Moldavia north of the Danube by the Sultan's leave. She had in her veins the blood of the Byzantine families of Palaiologos and Cantacuzene. She was related to the court of the Komnenoi at Trebizond. Yet at times she seemed to be more Slav than Greek. One of her achievements was to persuade the Sultan Mehmed in 1469 to allow the bones of St Ivan Rilski to be moved from the old Bulgarian capital of Trnovo to the great monastery which still bears his name at Rila in south-western Bulgaria, which had then been a Turkish province for about seventy years. There is some evidence that she maintained a workshop of scribes and artists at her court at Ježevo.[24] Her own talents, however, were more practical. It was in the promotion and furtherance of tolerance and good relations between Christians and Turks that Mara excelled. She put to the best possible use the favours and privileges granted to her by the enemies of her Orthodox faith.

She died at Ježevo on 14 September 1487 and was buried in the mon-

---

[23] Babinger, *Mehmed*, pp. 437–8; Runciman, *Great Church*, p. 194.
[24] *PLP*, VII, p. 141.

astery of the Virgin called Eikosiphoinissa at Kosinitza, to which her friend and confessor Dionysios had retired after his unhappy term as Patriarch.[25] She was not much over seventy. She had been a widow for thirty-six years. She had never married again. She had no children; and she resisted the temptation so common among ladies of her class to become a nun in her declining years. Her portrait as a young woman can be seen in the deed of gift (chrysobull) which her father George Branković granted to the monastery of Esphigmenou on Mount Athos in August 1429. She must then have been about fifteen. She is shown standing next to her stepmother Eirene Cantacuzene and her father and her three younger brothers, Gregory, Stephen and Lazar, in a stylised and not very realistic family group. The poses and the costumes of the figures emphasise that Mara was an outstanding example of that amalgam of Balkan peoples which has been called the Byzantine Commonwealth.[26]

A sixteenth-century chronicler summed her up in these words: 'The lady Mara was the wife of the Sultan Murad, the stepmother of the Sultan Mehmed, who gave her much landed property near Serres for her upkeep, including Ezova [Ježevo] and the neighbouring places, and there she lived like a princess in authority until the end of her life.'[27] She is not much remembered now. But in the township of Nigrita, the modern Ježevo, local lore commemorates her name. A ruined tower in the medieval walls is known as the Tower of the Lady Mara.[28]

---

[25] See F. Babinger, 'Witwensitz und Sterbeplatz der Sultanin Mara', *EEBS*, XXIII (1953), 240–4. The Victoria and Albert Museum possesses a pair of embroidered silk *epimanikia* (cuffs) of the sixteenth century which once belonged to an archimandrite of what was then 'the patriarchal monastery of Kozynitsa'. It may have been Mara's influence with the Turks that helped the monastery to survive and to be so specially privileged.

[26] V. J. Djurić, 'Portreti na poveljama vizantijskih i srpskih vladara', *Zbornik filosofskog fakulteta*, VII (Belgrade, 1963), fig. 15; reproduced in Nicol, *Byzantine Family of Kantakouzenos*, plate 11.

[27] *Ecthesis Chronica and Chronicon Athenarum*, ed. Sp. P. Lambros (London, 1902), p. 22.

[28] A. E. Vakalopoulos, *History of Macedonia 1354–1833* (Thessaloniki, 1973), pp. 119–21.

CHAPTER TEN

────────{⊃⊂}────────

HELENA CANTACUZENE KOMNENE,
EMPRESS OF TREBIZOND,
DIED c. 1463

HELENA, who became the last Empress of Trebizond, was a sister of
Eirene Cantacuzene, the first wife of George Branković, the Despot of
Serbia. She had three brothers and two sisters. They were the great-
grandchildren of the Emperor John VI Cantacuzene. One of her
brothers was that Thomas Cantacuzene whom Mara Branković claimed
as her uncle; another was George Palaiologos Cantacuzene, who, after a
distinguished career in the Morea (Peloponnese), settled in Serbia and
joined in the defence of Smederevo against the Turks. Trebizond on the
Black Sea was a very long way away from Smederevo on the Danube.
The half-way house was Byzantine Constantinople; and in the struggle
for survival against the expansion of the Ottoman Turks the links
between the houses of Branković and Cantacuzene and the ruling
family of Trebizond were many.[1]

Trebizond was the capital of an Empire which existed more in a
constitutional than a geographical sense. Territorially it consisted of a
long strip of coast along the southern shore of the Black Sea protected
from central Anatolia by the barrier of the Pontic mountains. Its wealth
and its influence were far from commensurate with its size and popu-
lation. By the year 1400 its rulers had called themselves Emperors for
two hundred years. They were Greek by language, Byzantine by
culture and tradition and Orthodox by faith. The true Emperors of the
Romans in Constantinople had obliged them to modify their imperial
claims by styling themselves Emperors of Anatolia or all the East. But
they were still Emperors with all that the title implied in the Byzantine
world, and they distinguished themselves by adopting the surname of
Grand Komnenos. This microcosm of a Byzantine Empire on the Black
Sea was constantly threatened by its powerful and unpredictable neigh-

[1] D. M. Nicol, *The Byzantine Family of Kantakouzenos (Cantacuzenus)* (Washington,
D. C., 1968), no. 72 (Helena), no. 71 (Eirene), no. 70 (Thomas), no. 67 (George).

bours, the Mongols and the Turks in the interior of Asia Minor. Their Emperors survived and prospered partly by making timely submissions or payments of tribute to their enemies and partly by arranging well-planned marriage alliances with their leaders, whether Christian or Muslim. Many of the Emperors of Trebizond were blessed with progenies of marriageable daughters; and the beauty of the ladies of Trebizond was as legendary as the richness of their dowries. Several of them were destined to keep the barbarian wolves at bay by marrying local Turkish Emirs or the more exotic chieftains of the nomad Turkoman tribes of the so-called Ak-koyunlu and Kara-koyunlu, the hordes of the White Sheep and the Black Sheep. Some of the Emperors, however, maintained the link with the real Byzantine world by marrying ladies of the imperial families of Palaiologos and Cantacuzene. Alexios III Grand Komnenos, who died in 1390, married Theodora Cantacuzene. Another Theodora Cantacuzene married Alexios IV of Trebizond in 1395. It was from this marriage that the last two Emperors of Trebizond were born.[2]

Theodora Cantacuzene presented her husband with three sons and three daughters, one of whom married the Emperor of Constantinople, John VIII. Her first son succeeded as Emperor in Trebizond as John IV when his father Alexios died in 1429. Her second son David became Emperor when his brother died in 1458. The Grand Komnenos David was the last of the line. He reigned for only three years. He came into a *damnosa haereditas*. The days of Christian Trebizond were numbered in 1458. Constantinople had fallen to the Turks five years before. In 1459 the conquering Sultan Mehmed II put an end to what was left of Christian Serbia. In 1460 he extinguished the last Byzantine light in Greece by capturing Mistra and taking over the Despotate of the Morea in the Peloponnese. The Emperor John IV of Trebizond had sensed that his own little Empire would be next on the Sultan's list for extinction. He planned a series of alliances with his neighbours to form a coalition of forces strong enough to fend off the Turks. His most powerful ally was the Lord of the White Sheep in Diyarbakir in Mesopotamia, Uzun Hasan, to whom he gave his daughter Theodora in marriage. His brother David, who succeeded him in 1458, dreamed of enlarging and strengthening the coalition by interesting the powers of the western

---

[2] On the Empire of Trebizond, see W. Miller, *Trebizond. The Last Greek Empire* (London, 1926; repr. Amsterdam, 1968); E. Janssens, *Trébizonde en Colchide* (Brussels, 1969). On Theodora and Alexios IV, see Nicol, *Byzantine Family of Kantakouzenos*, no. 61; A. Bryer, 'Ludovico da Bologna and the Georgian and Anatolian Embassy of 1460–1461', *Bedi Kartlisa: revue de kartvélologie*, xix–xx (1965), 178–98.

world in the fate of Trebizond, notably Pope Pius II and the Duke Philip of Burgundy. All of them were living in fantasy.[3]

Like his father and grandfather before him David Komnenos had married a lady of the Cantacuzene family. He had been married before, to a daughter of the Prince of Gotthia in the Crimea. But to have a Cantacuzene to wife was a step up in the pecking order of Byzantine aristocracy. The date of his marriage to Helena is not recorded. Judging from the number of children that she is said to have borne him it must have occurred at the latest about 1440. The proposal may well have emanated from Serbia, where Helena's brother George Palaiologos Cantacuzene had settled. George Branković, the Despot of Serbia, had first been married to a sister of John IV of Trebizond, David's elder brother. The known facts of Helena's brief career as Empress of Trebizond are few and derive only from chroniclers who lived long after her death and boasted some ancestral relationship with her family. The chronicle written by Michael Panaretos, the chief source for the history of the rulers of Trebizond, unfortunately ends with the reign of John IV and records only the first marriage of his brother David. The later Byzantine historians as well as a number of the so-called Short Chronicles record the circumstances of the Turkish conquest of Trebizond.[4] But the only account of the last years of Helena's life is that given by Theodore Spandounes in his history of the rise of the Ottoman Empire, produced in Italy in 1538. If his tales are true, the Empress Helena of Trebizond earned more fame in her death than ever she had in her life.

It was in 1460 that the Sultan Mehmed decided that the moment had come to incorporate into his dominions the last remnant of Byzantium by conquering Trebizond. The Emperor David was a weak and foolish man. He provoked the Sultan to fury by refusing to pay him the tribute which his late brother had been obliged to pay. The conquest of Trebizond was a major military operation conducted by sea and by land, with enormous numbers of troops and ships. Just before the siege began, David sent Helena out of harm's way to stay with his friend and relative the Lord of Guria in Georgia.[5] His most potent ally, Uzun Hasan, also provoked the Sultan's wrath. He thought it prudent to make a gesture of peace before surrender was forced upon him; and David, seeing that Trebizond was isolated, handed over the keys of the

---

[3] On John IV and his brother David, see *PLP*, v, nos. 12108, 12097. On Uzun Hasan, *PLP*, ix, no. 21157.

[4] The sources are listed in *Chronica byzantina breviora*, ed. P. Schreiner, *Die byzantinischen kleinchroniken* (Vienna, 1975–9), ii, pp. 499–500.

[5] Bryer, 'Ludovico da Bologna', 183.

city, in August 1461. The Byzantine Christian Empire of Trebizond was no more. Its last Emperor and his Empress Helena with their children were shipped to Constantinople to await the Sultan's pleasure when he returned to his capital.[6]

The number of Helena's children is variously recorded by the sources. Some give it as eight sons and one daughter. Others, more convincingly, write of three sons and one daughter, naming them as Basil, Manuel, George and Anna. When the Sultan got back to Constantinople he had them all moved to Adrianople and settled them there in reasonable comfort supported by landed estates in the Strymon valley near Serres. It is possible that he expected his stepmother Mara Branković, who lived in the same area and was their relative, to keep an eye on them. Two years later, however, David was accused of complicity in a plot against the Sultan and imprisoned with Helena and their children. Mehmed then concluded that the best way to ensure that the line of the last Byzantine claimants to the title of Emperor would not be perpetuated was to be rid of all the male members of the family of Grand Komnenos. They were moved to the prison of the Seven Towers in Constantinople and there, on 1 November 1463, the Emperor David with his three sons, his nephew and his brother-in-law were executed.[7]

Helena was allowed to survive. She declined to do so. The story of her tragic end is told by Theodore Spandounes, writing some seventy-five years after the event.[8] It may be over-dramatised but it may well be true. Spandounes himself was proud to be a Cantacuzene and related to Helena. He describes her as having been a sister of his grandmother. He was also a grandnephew of Mara Branković, who was still alive in 1463 and with whom he stayed at Ježevo as a young man.[9] It may have been from her that he heard the sad and moving tale of the Empress Helena's death. After their execution, Mehmed ordered that the corpses of David and his children should be thrown outside the walls of the city and left unburied to become prey for the dogs and crows. He confiscated all David's property and commanded Helena to pay him the sum of 15,000 ducats within the space of three days or suffer the same fate as her husband. Her retainers in Constantinople contrived to find the money

---

[6] Miller, *Trebizond*, pp. 97–108; Babinger, *Mehmed*, pp. 190–97.

[7] J. Enoch Powell, 'Die letzten Tage der Grosskomnenen', *BZ*, XXXVII (1937), 358–9. *PLP*, V, nos. 12057, 12091, 12093, 12112.

[8] Theodore Spandounes (Spandugnino), *De la origine deli Imperatori Ottomani*, ed. C. N. Sathas, *Documents inédits relatifs à l'histoire de la Grèce au moyen âge*, IX (Paris, 1890), pp. 159–60.

[9] Spandounes, p. 159 lines 21–2: 'Helena Cantacusina, sorella de mio avo materno'. On his relationship to Mara Branković, see above, pp. 116–17.

within twenty-four hours. She had no desire to remain in this world. But she had one last Christian duty to perform. She put on sackcloth, she who had been used to regal finery; she refused to eat; and she built herself a hovel covered with straw in which she slept rough beside the corpses of her husband and sons outside the city walls. The Sultan had decreed that they should not be buried. Helena outwitted him. Secretly she found a spade and with her own delicate hands dug a trench inside her hut. All day she defended the corpses against the animals and under cover of night took them one by one and gave them Christian burial. 'Thus did God give her the grace to bury her husband and her sons; and a few days later she died.' It is tragically appropriate that the last lady to bear the Byzantine title of Empress should have ended her days like Antigone.

The Sultan Mehmed did his work well. The imperial house of Grand Komnenos which had ruled Trebizond for more than 250 years was exterminated. On one day in 1463 Helena had lost her husband and her three surviving sons, Basil, Manuel and George, as well as her brother-in-law Alexander and her nephew Alexios. It is no wonder that she lost her own will to live. But she would not die until she had performed the last rites of a duteous widow and mother. Some say that she retreated into monastic seclusion before willingly surrendering her soul. The one survivor of her family was her daughter Anna. She was given as a wife to Zaganos Pasha, one of the Sultan's viziers. He got rid of her when she declined to disown her Christian faith and become a Muslim.[10] Helena's line was carried on only through her niece Theodora who had married Uzun Hasan. For her grandson was Ismail, the first of the Safavid Shahs of Persia whose descendants ruled until 1736.[11]

The imperial family of Grand Komnenos of Trebizond came to its bitter end with the massacre of the Emperor David and his offspring in 1463 and the death of his Empress Helena. The very last Byzantine lady to serve the moribund cause of her ancestors, however, was Zoe Palaiologina, a niece of the last Christian Emperor of Constantinople, Constantine XI. Being a daughter of Constantine's brother, Thomas Palaiologos, the last Despot of the Morea at Mistra, Zoe had in her veins the blood of almost all of the ruling families of the final shreds and patches

---

[10] *PLP*, III, no. 6415; V, no. 12057.

[11] Nicol, *Byzantine Family of Kantakouzenos*, no. 72 requires considerable revision on Helena's family and descendants. See now M. Kuršanskis, 'Relations matrimoniales entre Grands Comnènes de Trébizonde et princes géorgiens', *Bedi Kartlisa*, XXIV (1972), 112–27; Kuršanskis, 'La descendance d'Alexis IV Empereur de Trébizonde', *REB*, XXXVII (1979), 239–47. R. M. Savory, in *Encyclopaedia of Islam²*, IV (1978), pp. 186–8.

of the Byzantine world in the fifteenth century. She was related to the houses of Cantacuzene, of Palaiologos, of Branković, of Asen, and of Komnenos of Trebizond. The hope that such well-connected ladies could, through judicious intermarriage, solve the international problems caused by the territorial and other ambitions of their menfolk was persistent. The possibilities of exploiting the young Zoe Palaiologina were realised not by an Emperor or a Despot, for none such existed after the fall of Trebizond in 1461. When her father Thomas fled from Mistra in 1460, he took his family as refugees to Rome; and there the Pope, Sixtus IV, arranged for Zoe to marry Ivan III, Grand Prince of Moscow. She was to be his agent for the conversion of the Russians to Roman Catholicism. The Pope provided her dowry and solemnised her betrothal to Ivan III in Rome in 1472. She was then sixteen. The Russians, however, declined to be converted; and her wedding was celebrated in Moscow according to the Byzantine Orthodox rite of her ancestors. Her husband and his people called her Sophia. He was the first Russian prince to adopt the title of Tsar, the Slav equivalent of Emperor. He also adopted as his emblem of state the late Byzantine device of the double-headed eagle. But these minor manifestations of Byzantine imperialism need not be credited to the influence of his young wife Zoe-Sophia. She served her husband faithfully. She gave him four sons. Her grandson was Ivan IV the Terrible. She died in 1503. The last Byzantine lady cannot therefore be held responsible for engendering the later Russian fantasy that Moscow was the Third Rome of the Christian world.[12]

---

[12] Obolensky, *The Byzantine Commonwealth* (London, 1971), pp. 363–4; D. M. Nicol, *The Immortal Emperor. The life and legend of Constantine Palaiologos, last Emperor of the Romans* (Cambridge, 1992), p. 115.

BIBLIOGRAPHY

SOURCES

Akropolites, George, *Historia. Georgii Acropolitae Opera*, ed. A. Heisenberg, 1 (Leipzig, 1903); ed. P. Wirth (Stuttgart, 1978)

Anonymus Tranensis (Anonymous of Trani), *Dissertazione sulla seconda moglie del Re Manfredi e su' loro figlioli*, ed. D. Forges-Davanzati (Naples, 1791)

Athanasios I, Patriarch, *Letters. The Correspondence of Athanasius I Patriarch of Constantinople. Letters to the Emperor Andronicus II, Members of the Imperial Family, and Officials*, ed. Alice-Mary Maffry Talbot (*CFHB*, VII: Washington, D.C. 1975)

Barišić, F., 'Povelje vizantijskich carica', *ZRVI*, XIII (1971), 143–202

Benedict XII, Pope, *Acta Benedicti XII (1334–1342)*, ed. A. L. Tautu (Vatican City, 1958)

Bertelè, T., *Monetè e sigilli di Anna di Savoia, imperatrice di Bisanzio* (Rome, 1937)

Boissonade, J. F., *Anecdota Graeca*, 5 vols. (Paris, 1829–33)
Anecdota Nova (Paris, 1844)

Cantacuzene (Kantakouzenos), John, *History. Ioannis Cantacuzeni eximperatoris Historiarum Libri IV*, ed. L. Schopen, 3 vols. (*CSHB*, 1828–32)

Chalkokondyles, *Historiae*, ed. E. Darkó, *Laonici Chalcocandylae Historiarum Demonstrationes*, 2 vols. (Budapest, 1922–7)

Choumnaina, Eirene-Eulogia, *Correspondence*, ed. Angela Constantinides Hero, *A Woman's Quest for Spiritual Guidance. The correspondence of Princess Irene Eulogia Choumnaina Palaiologina* (Brookline, Mass., 1986)

Choumnos, Nikephoros, *Letters*, ed. J. F. Boissonade, *Anecdota Graeca*, I (Paris, 1829); *Anecdota nova*, (Paris, 1844); ed. P. M. L. Leone, *EEBS*, XXXIX–XL (1972–3), 75–95

Chronica byzantina breviora, ed. P. Schreiner, *Die byzantinischen Kleinchroniken*, (*CFHB*, XII, 1–3: Vienna, 1975–9)

Clement V, Pope, *Les registres de Clément V* ed. E. Jordan, (Paris, 1893–1945)

Clement VI, Pope, *Letters*, ed. E. Déprez, *Clément VI (1242–1252), Lettres closes, patentes et curiales publiées ou analysées d'après les registres du Vatican* (Paris, 1901–25)

Cognasso, F., 'Una crisobolla di Michele IX Paleologo per Teodoro I di Monferrato', *Studi Bizantini*, II (1927), 38–47

Constantine Porphyrogenitus, *De Administrando Imperio*, ed. and trans. R. J. H. Jenkins and Gy. Moravcsik, 2nd ed. (*CFHB* I: Washington, D.C., 1967)

Doukas (Ducas), *Istoria Turco-Bizantină (1341–1462)*, ed. V. Grecu (Bucharest, 1958); trans. H. J. Magoulias, Doukas. *Decline and Fall of Byzantium to the Ottoman Turks* (Detroit, 1975)

Ekthesis Chronike, ed. Sp. P. Lambros, *Ecthesis Chronica and Chronicon Athenarum* (London, 1902)

Filelfo, Francesco, ed. E. Legrand, *Cent-dix lettres grecques de François Filelfe* (Paris, 1892)

Gouillard, J., 'Le Synodikon de l'Orthodoxie. Edition et commentaire', *TM*, II (1967), 1–313

Gregoras, Nikephoros, *History. Byzantina Historia*, ed. L. Schopen, 3 vols. (*CSHB*, 1829–55)

Gregory of Cyprus, *Letters*, ed. S. Eustratiades, in *EPh*, I (1908), II (1908); III (1909); IV (1909); V (1910)

Guillou, A., *Les archives de Saint-Jean Prodrome sur le mont Ménécée* (Paris, 1955)

Hyrtakenos, Theodore, *Letters*, ed. J. F. Boissonade, *Anecdota Graeca*, I (Paris, 1829)

John XXII, Pope, *Acta Ioannis XXII (1317–1334)*, ed. A. L. Tautu (Vatican City, 1952)

Kritoboulos of Imbros, ed. V. Grecu (Bucharest, 1963); ed. D. Reinsch (*CFHB*, XXII: Berlin–New York, 1983)

Lamansky, V., *Secrets d'état de Venise. Documents extraits notices et études servant à éclaircir les rapports de la Seigneurie avec les Grecs et les Slaves et la Porte Ottomane à la fin du XVe et au XVIe siècle* (St Petersburg, 1884)

Lampenos, Alexios, *Monodies*, ed. Sp. P. Lambros, *NE*, XI (1914), 359–400

Leone, P. L. M., 'Le epistole di Niceforo Chumno nel cod. Ambros. gr. 71 sup.', *EEBS*, XXXIX–XL (1972–3), 75–95

Libro de los Fechos et Conquistas del Principado de la Morea, ed. A. Morel-Fatio (Geneva, 1885)

Livre de la Conquête de la Princée de l'Amorée. Chronique de Morée, ed. J. Longnon (Paris, 1911)

Manuel II Palaiologos, *Dialogue. Manuel Palaiologos. Dialogue with the Empress Mother on marriage. Introduction, text and translation* by A. Angelou (Byzantina Vindobonensia, 19: Vienna, 1989)

Matthew of Ephesos, Bishop, *Letters*, ed. D. Reinsch, *Die Briefe des Matthaios von Ephesus im Codex Vindobonensis Theol. Gr. 174* (Berlin, 1974)

Meyer, Ph., 'Bruchstücke zweier τυπικὰ κτητορικά', *BZ* IV (1895), 45–58

Migne, J. P. *Patrologiae Cursus Completus. Series Graeco-Latina* (Paris, 1857–66) [= *MPG*]

Miklosich, F. and Müller, J. *Acta et Diplomata graeca medii aevi sacra et profana*, 6 vols. (Vienna, 1860–90) [= *MM*]

Moschos, John, ed. E. Legrand, "Ἰωάννου τοῦ Μόσχου Λόγος Ἐπιτάφιος ἐπὶ τοῦ Λ. Νοταρᾶ,' *DIEE*, II (1885–6), 413–24

Pachymeres, George, *History*. *De Michaele et Andronico Palaeologis*, ed. I. Bekker, 2 vols. (*CSHB*, 1835); new ed. in progress: *Pachymères, Georges, Relations historiques*, ed. A. Failler, trans. V. Laurent (*CFHB*, XXIV: Paris, 1984–)

Papadopoulos-Kerameus, A., Ἀνάλεκτα Ἱεροσολυμιτικῆς Σταχυολογίας, 5 vols. (St Petersburg, 1891–8)

Papadopoulos-Kerameus, A., Ἱεροσολυμιτικὴ Βιβλιοθήκη, 4 vols. (St Petersburg, 1891–9)

Pertusi, A., ed. *La caduta di Costantinopoli*, I: *Le testimonianze dei contemporanei*; II: *L'eco nel mondo* (Fondazione Lorenzo Valla: Verona, 1976)

Philes, Manuel, *Poems*, ed. E. Miller, *Manuelis Philae Carmina*, 2 vols. (Paris, 1855, 1857); Ae. Martini, *Manuelis Philae Carmina Inedita* (Naples, 1900)

Pius II, Pope, *Commentaries of Pius II*, trans. Florence A. Gragg, ed. Leona Gabel (London, 1960)

Planoudes, Maximos, *Epigrams*, ed. Sp. P. Lambros, *NE*, XIII (1916), 414–21

Planoudes, Maximos, *Letters*, ed. M. Treu, *Maximi monachi Planudis epistulae* (Breslau, 1890)

Previale, L., 'Due monodie inedite di Matteo di Efeso', *BZ*, XLI (1941), 4–34

Pseudo-Kodinos, *De Officiis*, ed. J. Verpeaux, *Pseudo-Kodinos, Traité des Offices* (Paris, 1966)

Pseudo-Phrantzes, *Chronicon minus*. (*see* Sphrantzes, George)

Ptolemy of Lucca. *Ptolomaei Lucensis Historia Ecclesiastica*, ed. L. A. Muratori, *Rerum Italicarum Scriptores*, XI (Milan 1727)

Salaville, S., 'Une lettre et un discours inédits de Théolepte de Philadelphie', *REB*, V (1947), 101–15

Sanuto, Marino, *Diarii*, ed. R. Fulin, VII (Venice, 1882)

Sathas, C. N., Μνημεῖα Ἑλληνικῆς Ἱστορίας. *Documents inédits relatifs à l'histoire de la Grèce au moyen âge*, IX (Paris, 1890)

Spandounes. *Theodoro Spandugnino, Patritio Constantinopolitano, De origine deli Imperatori Ottomani, ordine dela corte forma del guerreggiare loro, religione, rito, et costumi dela natione*, ed. C. N. Sathas, Μνημεῖα Ἑλληνικῆς Ἱστορίας. *Documents inédits relatifs à l'histoire de la Grèce au moyen âge*, IX (Paris, 1890); partial French paraphrase by C. Schefer, *Petit traicté de l'origine des Turcqz par Théodore Spandouyn Cantacasin* (Paris, 1896)

Sphrantzes, George, *Chronicon minus*. *Georgios Sphrantzes, Memorii 1401–1477. In anexă Pseudo-Phrantzes: Macarie Melissenos, Cronica 1258–1481*, ed. V. Grecu (Bucharest, 1966)

Westerink, L. G., 'Nikephoros Gregoras, Dankrede an die Mutter Gottes', *Helikon*, VII (1967), 259–71 (reprinted in Westerink, *Texts and Studies in Neoplatonism and Byzantine Literature* (Amsterdam, 1980), pp. 229–41)

MODERN WORKS

Abrahamse, Dorothy de F., 'Women's monasticism in the Middle Byzantine period: problems and prospects', *BF*, IX (1985), 35–58

BIBLIOGRAPHY

Babinger, F., 'Ein Freibrief Medmeds II, der Eroberers, für das Kloster Hagia Sophia zu Saloniki, Eigentum des Sultanin Mara (1459)', *BZ*, XLIV (1951), 11–20

Babinger, F., *Mehmed the Conqueror and his Time*, trans. R. Mannheim, ed. W. C. Hickman (Princeton, N.J., 1978)

Babinger, F., 'Witwensitz und Sterbeplatz der Sultanin Mara', *EEBS*, XXIII (1953), 240–4

Barišić, F., 'Povelje vizantijskich carica [Les chartes des impératrices byzantines]', *ZRVI*, XIII (1971), 143–202

Barker, J. W., 'The problem of Byzantine appanages during the Palaeologan period', *Byzantina*, III, (1971), 103–22

Belting, H., *Das illuminierte Buch in der spätbyzantinischen Gesellschaft* (Heidelberg, 1970)

Bendall, S. and Donald, P. J., *The Later Palaeologan Coinage* (London, 1979)

Berg, B. 'Manfred of Sicily and the Greek East', *Byzantina*, XIV (1988), 263–89

Beyer, H.-V. 'Eine Chronologie der Lebensgeschichte des Nikephoros Gregoras', *JÖB*, XXVII (1978), 127–55

Bosch, Ursula V., *Kaiser Andronikos III. Palaiologos. Versuch einer Darstellung der byzantinischen Geschichte in den Jahren 1321 1341* (Amsterdam, 1965)

Božilov, I., *Familijata na Asenevci (1186–1460). Genealogija i prosopografija* (Sofia, 1985)

Brown, H., *The Venetian Printing Press 1469–1800* (London, 1891; rep. Amsterdam, 1969)

Bryer, A. A. M., 'Greek historians on the Turks: the case of the first Byzantine–Ottoman marriage', in *The Writing of History in the Middle ages. Essays presented to R. W. Southern*, ed. R. H. C. Davis and J. M. Wallace-Hadrill (Oxford, 1981), pp. 471–93

Bryer, A., 'Lodovico da Bologna and the Georgian and Anatolian Embassy of 1460–1461', *Bedi Kartlisa: revue de kartvélologie*, XIX–XX (1965), 178–98

Buchthal, H. and Belting, H., *Patronage in Thirteenth-Century Constantinople. An atelier of Late Byzantine book illumination and calligraphy* (Dumbarton Oaks Studies, XVI: Washington, D.C., 1978)

Caggese, R., *Roberto d'Angiò e i suoi tempi*, I (Florence, 1922)

Canart, P. and Peri, V., *Sussidi Bibliografici per i manoscritti greci della Biblioteca Vaticana* (Studi e Testi, 261: Vatican City, 1970)

Cecchini, G., Anna Notara Paleologa. Una principessa greca in Italia e la politica senese di ripopolamento della Maremma', *Bulletino Senese di Storia Patria*, n.s. IX (1938), 1–41

Chatzes, A. Ch., Οἱ Ῥαούλ, Ῥάλ, Ῥάλαι *(1080–1800)* (Kirchhain, 1909)

Chatzidakis, M., *Icônes de Saint-Georges des Grecs et de la Collection de l'Institut*, Bibliothèque de l'Institut hellénique d'Etudes Byzantines et Post-Byzantines de Venise, I (Venice, 1962); VIII (Venice, 1975)

Christophilopoulou, Aikaterina, Ἡ ἀντιβασιλεία εἰς τὸ Βυζάντιον, Σύμμεικτα, II (1970), 1–144

Chrysostomides, Julian, 'Italian women in Greece in the late fourteenth and early fifteenth centuries', *Rivista di Studi Bizantini e Slavi*, II (= *Miscellanea Agostino Pertusi*, II) (1982), 119–32

Constantinides, C., *Higher Education in Byzantium in the Thirteenth and Early Fourteenth Centuries (1204 – ca. 1310)* (Nicosia, 1982)

Constantinidi-Bibikou, Hélène, 'Documents concernant l'histoire Byzantine déposés aux archives nationales de France', *Mélanges offerts à Octave et Melpo Merlier*, I (Athens, 1960), 119–32

Constantinidi-Bibikou, Hélène, 'Yolande de Montferrat impératrice de Byzance', *L'Hellénisme Contemporain*, 2nd series, IV (1950), 425–42

Darrouzès, J., 'Autres manuscrits originaires de Chypre', *REB*, XV (1957), 156

Del Giudice, G., *Codice Diplomatico di Carlo I e II di Angiò, 1265–1309*, 2 vols. (Naples, 1863–1902)

Del Giudice, G., 'La famiglia di Re Manfredi', *ASPN*, III (1878), 3–80; IV (1879), 35–110, 290–362; V (1880), 21–95, 262–323, 470–547. Also printed separately (Naples, 1896)

Dendias, M. A., Ἑλένη Ἀγγελίνα Δούκαινα Βασίλισσα Σικελίας καὶ Νεαπόλεως, Ἠπειρωτικὰ Χρονικά, I (1926), 219–94

Devreesse, R., *Bibliothèque Nationale. Catalogue des manuscrits grecs*, II: *Le fond Coislin* (Paris, 1945)

Diehl, C., *Figures Byzantines*, series I–II (Paris, 1906–8)

Diehl, C., *Impératrices de Byzance* (Paris, 1959)

Diehl, C., 'Anne de Savoie, femme d'Andronic III', *Figures byzantines*, II, 245–65 (= Diehl, *Impératrices de Byzance*, pp. 275–95)

Diehl, C., 'Constance de Hohenstaufen Impératrice de Nicée', in Diehl, *Figures byzantines*, II, 207–25

Diehl, C., 'Princesses d'Occident à la cour des Comnènes', in Diehl, *Figures byzantines*, II, 164–206

Djurić, I., 'Pomenik Svetogorskog Protata c kraja XIV veka' (Mémorial du Protaton de Mont Athos à la fin du XIVe siècle), *ZRVI*, XX (1981), 139–69

Djurić, V. J., 'Portreti na poveljama vizantijskih i srpskih vladara', *Zbornik filosofskog fakulteta*, VII (Belgrade, 1963), 251–72 [Portraits des souverains byzantins et serbes sur les chrysobulles]

Dölger, F., *Aus dem Schatzkammern des Heiligen Berges*, 2 vols. (Munich, 1948)

Dölger, F., *Facsimiles byzantinischer Kaiserurkunden* (Munich, 1931)

Dölger, F., *Regesten der Kaiserurkunden des oströmischen Reiches*, III: *1204–1282* (2nd ed. P. Wirth: Munich, 1977); IV: *1282–1341*; V: *1341–1453* (Munich-Berlin, 1924–65) (= *DR*)

Dölger, F., 'Zum Kaisertum der Anna von Savoyen', in Dölger, *PARASPORA. 30 Aufsätze zur Geschichte, Kultur und Sprache des byzantinischen Reiches* (Ettal, 1961), pp. 208–21

Failler, A., 'Nouvelle note sur la chronologie du règne de Jean Cantacuzène', *REB*, XXXIV (1976), 119–24

Fassoulakis, S., *The Byzantine Family of Raoul Ral(l)es* (Athens, 1973)

Fedalto, G., *Ricerche storiche sulla posizione giuridiche ed ecclesiastica dei Greci a Venezia nei secoli XV e XVI* (Florence, 1967)

Filangieri, R. *I Registri della Cancelleria Angioina*, ricostruiti da Riccardo Filangieri (Naples, 1950–) (in progress)

Fonkić, B. L., 'Zametki o grečeskich rukopisjach Sovietskich chranilišč', *VV*, XXXVI (1974), 134–8

Garland, Lynda, 'The life and ideology of Byzantine women. A further note on the conventions of behaviour and social reality as reflected in eleventh and twelfth century historical sources', *B*, LVIII (1988), 361–93

Gay, J., *Le pape Clément VI et les affaires d'Orient (1342–1352)* (Paris, 1904)

Geanakoplos, D. J., *Emperor Michael Palaeologus and the West 1258–1282. A study in Byzantine–Latin relations* (Cambridge, Mass., 1959)

Geanakoplos, D. J., 'The Greco–Byzantine colony in Venice and its significance in the Renaissance', in Geanakoplos, *Byzantine East and Latin West* (Oxford, 1966), pp. 112–37

Geanakoplos, D. J., *Greek Scholars in Venice. Studies in the dissemination of Greek learning from Byzantium to Western Europe* (Cambridge, Mass., 1962)

Gill, J., *Byzantium and the Papacy, 1198–1400* (New Brunswick, N.J., 1979)

Gill, J., 'Matrons and brides of fourteenth-century Byzantium', *BF*, X (1985), 39–56

Grabar, A., 'Une pyxide en ivoire à Dumbarton Oaks. Quelques notes sur l'art profane pendant les derniers siècles de l'Empire byzantin', *DOP*, XIV (1960), 121–46

Hero, Angela C., 'Irene-Eulogia Choumnaina Palaiologina Abbess of the Convent of Philanthropos Soter in Constantinople', *BF*, IX (1985), 119–47

Hero, Angela C., 'The unpublished letters of Theoleptos Metropolitan of Philadelphia (1283–1322)', *Journal of Modern Hellenism*, II (1986), 1–31; IV (1987), 1–17.

Hero, Angela Constantinides, *A Woman's Quest for Spiritual Guidance: The correspondence of Princess Irene Eulogia Choumnaina Palaiologina* (Brookline, Mass., 1986)

Hunger, H., *Schreiben und Lesen in Byzanz. Die byzantinische Buchkultur* (Munich, 1989)

Hunger, H. and Kresten, O., 'Archaisirende Minuskel und Hodegonstil im 14. Jahrhundert. Der Schreiber Theoktistos und die κράλαινα τῶν Τριβαλῶν', *JÖB*, XXIX (1980), 187–236

Janin, R., *Constantinople byzantine. Développement urbain et répertoire topographique*, 2nd ed. (Paris, 1964)

Janin, R., *Les églises et les monastères des grandes centres byzantines: Bithynie, Hellespont, Latros, Galèsios, Trébizonde, Athènes, Thessalonique* (Paris, 1975)

Janin, R., *La géographie ecclésiastique de l'empire byzantin, I: Le siège de Constantinople et le patriarche oecuménique; III: Les églises et les monastères des grands centres byzantins*, 2nd ed. (Paris, 1969)

Janin, R., 'Les monastères du Christ Philanthrope à Constantinople', *REB*, IV (1946), 153–62

Janssens, E., *Trébizonde en Colchide* (Brussels, 1969)

Jorga, N., 'Latins et grecs d'Orient et l'établissement des Turcs en Europe, 1342–62', *BZ*, xv (1906), 179–222

Kerofilas, C., *Une famille patricienne Crétoise. Les Vlasto* (New York, 1932)

Kotsonis, K. I., Λουκᾶς ὁ Νοταρᾶς ὁ πρῶτος ἐθνομάρτυς, 'Ακτῖνες, 189 (June, 1953), 1–24

Kourousis, S. I. Μανουὴλ-Ματθαῖος Γαβαλᾶς, I (Athens, 1972)

Koutibas, S. A., Οἱ Νοταράδες στὴν ὑπηρεσία τοῦ ἔθνους καὶ τῆς ἐκκλησίας (Athens, 1968)

Kugéas, S. 'Zur Geschichte der Münchener Thukydideshandschrift Augustanus F', *BZ*, xvi (1907), 61–2

Kuršanskis, M., 'La descendance d'Alexis IV Empereur de Trébizonde', *REB*, xxxvii (1979), 239–47

Kuršanskis, M., 'Relations matrimoniales entre Grands Comnènes de Trébizonde et princes géorgiens', *Bedi Kartlisa: revue de kartvélologie*, xxxiv (1972), 112–27

Kyrris, C. P., 'Le rôle de la femme dans la société byzantine pendant les derniers siècles', *JÖB*, xxxii, 2 (1982), 463–72

Laiou, Angeliki E., 'A Byzantine prince latinized: Theodore Palaeologus, Marquis of Montferrat', *B*, xxxviii (1968), 386–410.

Laiou, Angeliki E., 'The Byzantine aristocracy in the Palaeologan period: a story of arrested development', *Viator*, iv (1973), 131–51

Laiou, Angeliki E., *Constantinople and the Latins. The foreign policy of Andronicus II, 1282–1328* (Cambridge, Mass., 1972)

Laiou, Angeliki, E., 'Observations on the life and ideology of Byzantine women', *BF*, ix (1985), 59–102

Laiou, Angeliki, E., 'The role of women in Byzantine society', *XVI. Internationaler Byzantinistenkongress. Wien 1981, Akten*, i, 1 (= *JÖB*, 31/1) (Vienna, 1981), 233–60)

Lambros, Sp. P., Δύο Ἑλληνίδες βιβλιογράφοι, *NE*, x (1913), 347–8

Lambros, Sp. P., Κωνσταντῖνος Παλαιολόγος ὡς σύζυγος 'εν τῇ ἱστορίᾳ καὶ τοῖς θρύλοις, *NE*, iv (1907), 417–66

Lameere, W., *La tradition manuscrite de la correspondance de Grégoire de Chypre, patriarche de Constantinople (1283–1289)* (Brussels–Rome, 1937)

Laskaris, M., *Vizantiske prinzese u srednevekovnoj Srbiji* (Belgrade, 1926)

Laurent, V., 'La direction spirituelle à Byzance. La correspondance d'Irène-Eulogie Choumnaina Paléologue avec son second directeur', *REB*, xiv (1956), 48–86

Laurent, V., 'Les grandes crises religieuses à Byzance. La fin du schisme arsénite', *Académie roumaine. Bulletin de la section historique*, xxvi (1945), 225–313

Laurent, V., 'Une princesse byzantine au cloître. Irène-Eulogie Choumnos Paléologue, fondatrice du couvent de femmes τοῦ Φιλανθρώπου Σωτῆρος', *EO*, xxix (1930), 29–60

Laurent, V., *Les régestes des actes des patriarches de Constantinople*, i: *Les actes des patriarches*; iv *(1208–1309)* (Paris, 1971)

Legrand, E., *Bibliographie hellénique, ou description raisonnée des ouvrages en grec publiés par des Grecs au XV* *et XVI* *siècle*, 1 (Paris, 1885)

Lemerle, P., ed., *Actes de Kutlumus* (*Archives de l'Athos*, II² (Paris, 1988))

Lemerle, P., *L'Emirat d'Aydin, Byzance et l'Occident. Recherches sur 'La geste d'Umur Pacha'* (Paris, 1957)

Lemerle, P., *Philippes et la Macédoine orientale* (Paris, 1945)

Léonard, E. G., *Les Angevins de Naples* (Paris, 1954)

Loenertz, R.-J., 'Chronologie de Nicolas Cabasilas 1345–1354', *OCP*, XXXI (1955), 205–31 (= Loenertz, *Byzantina et Franco-Graeca*, 1 (Rome, 1970), 303–28).

Loenertz, R.-J., 'Mémoire d'Ogier, protonotaire, pour Marco et Marchetto nonces de Michel VIII Paléologue auprès du Pape Nicholas III. 1276 printemps–été', *OCP*, XXXI (1965), 374–408

Longnon, J., *L'Empire latin de Constantinople et la principauté de Morée.* (Paris, 1949)

Macrides, Ruth, 'Dowry and inheritance in the late period. some cases from the Patriarchal Register', in *Eherecht und Familiengut in Antike und Mittelalter*, ed. D. Simon (Oldenbourg, 1991), pp. 89–98

Macrides, Ruth, 'Dynastic marriages and political kinship', in *Byzantine Diplomacy*, ed. J. Shepard and S. Franklin (Variorum: Aldershot, 1992), pp. 263–80

Macrides, Ruth, 'Saints and sainthood in the early Palaiologan period', in *The Byzantine Saint*, ed. S. Hackel, Studies supplementary to *Sobornost*, V (1981), 67–87

Manoussakas, M. I., Ἡ πρώτη ἄδεια (1456) τῆς βενετικῆς γερουσιάς γιὰ τὸν ναὸν τῶν Ἑλλήνων τῆς Βενετιάς καὶ ὁ καρδινάλιος Ἰσίδωρος, *Thesaurismata*, 1 (1962), 109–18

Manoussakas, M. L., 'Recherches sur la vie de Jean Plousiadénos (Joseph de Méthone 1429?–1500)', *REB*, XVII (1959), 41–3

Manoussakas, M. I. and Paliouras, A. D., Ὁδηγὸς τοῦ Μουσείου τῶν Εἰκόνων καὶ τοῦ Ναοῦ τοῦ Ἁγίου Γεωργίου (Venice, 1976)

Manoussakas, M. and Staikos, K., ed., *The Publishing Activity of the Greeks during the Italian Renaissance* (Benaki Museum: Athens, 1987)

Marava-Chatzinikolaou, Anna and Touphexi-Paschou, Christina, Κατάλογος Μικρογραφικῶν Βυζαντινῶν Χειρογράφων τῆς Ἐθνικῆς Βιβλιοθήκης τῆς Ἑλλάδος, II (Athens, 1985)

Marinesco, C., 'Du nouveau sur Constance de Hohenstaufen, impératrice de Nicée', *B*, 1 (1924), 451–68

Maxwell, Kathleen, 'Another lectionary of the "atelier" of the Palaiologina, Vat. Gr. 532', *DOP*, XXXVII (1983), 47–54

Merendino, E., 'Manfredi tra Epiro e Nicea', *Actes du XV* *Congrès International d'Etudes byzantines*, IV (Athens, 1980), 245–52

Mertzios, K. D., Ἡ Διαθήκη τῆς Ἄννας Παλαιολογίνας Νοταρᾶ, *Athena*, LIII (1949), 17–21

Meyendorff, J., *Introduction à l'étude de Grégoire Palamas* (Paris, 1959)

Miller, W., *Trebizond. The last Greek Empire* (London, 1926; repr., Amsterdam, 1968)

Moschonas, N. G., 'I greci a Venezia e la loro posizione religiosa nel XVe secolo', *Eranistis*, v (1967), 105–37

Muratore, D., *Una principessa Sabauda sul trono di Bisanzio. Giovanna di Savoia Imperatrice Anna Paleologina*, Mémoires de l'Académie des sciences, belles-lettres et arts de Savoie, 4th ser., XI (Chambéry, 1909), 221–475

Nelson, R. S. and Lowden, J., 'The Palaeologina Group. Additional manuscripts and new questions', *DOP*, XLV (1991), 59–68

Nicol, D. M., *The Byzantine Family of Kantakouzenos (Cantacuzenus) ca. 1100–1460. A genealogical and prosopographical study* (Dumbarton Oaks Studies, XI: Washington, D.C., 1968)

Nicol, D. M., 'The Byzantine reaction to the Second Council of Lyons, 1274', in *Studies in Church History*, VII, ed. C. J. Cuming and D. Baker (Cambridge, 1971), pp. 113–46 (= Nicol, *Collected Studies* I, no. VI)

Nicol, D. M., *Byzantium and Venice. A study in diplomatic and cultural relations* (Cambridge, 1988)

Nicol, D. M., *Collected Studies*, I: *Byzantium: its ecclesiastical history and relations with the western world* (London, 1972)

Nicol, D. M., *Collected Studies*, II: *Studies in Late Byzantine History and Prosopography* (London, 1986)

Nicol, D. M., 'The date of the death of Nikephoros I of Epiros', *Rivista di Studi Bizantini e Slavi*, I (1981), 251–7

Nicol, D. M., *The Despotate of Epiros*, I: *1204–1267* (Oxford, 1957)

Nicol, D. M., *The Despotate of Epiros*, II: *1267–1479. A contribution to the history of Greece in the middle ages* (Cambridge, 1984)

Nicol, D. M., 'The Greeks and the union of the Churches: The report of Ogerius, protonotarius of Michael VIII Palaiologos', in Nicol, *Collected Studies* I, no. VII

Nicol, D. M., *The Immortal Emperor. The life and legend of Constantine Palaiologos, last Emperor of the Romans* (Cambridge, 1992)

Nicol, D. M., *The Last Centuries of Byzantium, 1261–1453*, 2nd edn (Cambridge, 1993)

Nicol D. M., 'Mixed marriages in Byzantium in the thirteenth century', in *Studies in Church History*, I, ed. C. W. Dugmore and C. Duggan (London and Edinburgh, 1964), 160–74 (= Nicol, *Collected Studies*, I, no. IV)

Nicol, D. M., 'The relations of Charles of Anjou with Nikephoros of Epiros', *BF*, IV (1972), 170–94 (= Nicol, *Collected Studies* II, no. V)

Nicol, D. M., 'Symbiosis and integration. Some Greco-Latin families in Byzantium in the 11th to 13th centuries', *BF*, VII (1979), 113–35 (= Nicol, *Collected Studies*, II, no. III)

Nicol, D. M., 'Thomas Despot of Epiros and the foundation date of the Paregoritissa at Arta', *Byzantina*, XIII, 2 (1985), 171–8

Nicol, D. M. and Bendall, S., 'Anna of Savoy in Thessalonica: the numismatic evidence', *Revue Numismatique*, 6th ser., XIX (1977), 87–102

Obolensky, D., *The Byzantine Commonwealth* (London, 1971)

Papadakis, A., *Crisis in Byzantium. The Filioque controversy in the Patriarchate of Gregory II of Cyprus (1283–1289)* (New York, 1983)

Papadopulos, A. Th., *Versuch einer Genealogie der Palaiologen 1259–1453* (Munich, 1938; repr. Amsterdam, 1962)

Parisot, V., *Cantacuzène homme d'état et historien* (Paris, 1845)

Pisani, P., 'Les chrétiens de rite oriental à Venise et dans les possessions vénitiennes (1438–1471)', *Revue d'histoire et de littérature religieuses*, I (1896), 201–24

Politis, L., 'Eine Schreiberschule im Kloster τῶν 'Οδηγῶν', *BZ*, LI (1958), 17–36, 261–87

Powell, J. Enoch, 'Die letzten Tage der Grosskomnenen', *BZ*, XXXVII (1937), 358–9

Prinzing, G., 'Sozialgeschichte der Frau im Spiegel der Chomatenos-Akten', *JÖB*, XXXII, 2 (1982), 453–62

Proctor, R., *The Printing of Greek in the Fifteenth Century* (Oxford, 1900)

Prosopographisches Lexikon der Palaiologenzeit, ed. E. Trapp et al. (Vienna, 1976f) (= *PLP*)

Protonotarios, P., 'John V and Anna of Savoy (1351–1365). The Serres hoard' (in Greek and English), *Nomismatika Chronika*, VIII (1989), 69–84

Runciman, S., *The Fall of Constantinople 1453* (Cambridge, 1965)

Runciman, S., *The Great Church in Captivity. A study of the Patriarchate of Constantinople from the eve of the Turkish conquest to the Greek War of Independence* (Cambridge, 1968)

Runciman, S., 'The marriages of the Sons of the Emperor Manuel II', *Rivista di Studi Bizantini e Slavi*, I (*Miscellanea Agostino Pertusi*: Bologna, 1981), 273–82

Runciman, S., *The Sicilian Vespers* (Cambridge, 1958)

Runciman, S., 'Thessalonica and the Montferrat inheritance', *Gregorios o Palamas*, XLII (1959), 27–34

Schlumberger, G. 'Le tombeau d'une impératrice Byzantine à Valence en Espagne', *Byzance et Croisades. Pages médiévales* (Paris, 1927), 56–86

Setton, K. M., *The Papacy and the Levant (1204–1571)*, I: *The Thirteenth and Fourteenth Centuries* (Philadelphia, 1976)

Ševčenko, I., 'Theodore Metochites, the Chora and the intellectual trends of his time', in *The Kariye Djami*, ed. P. Underwood IV (Princeton, N.J., 1975), pp. 19–91

Ševčenko, I., *La vie intellectuelle et politique à Byzance sous les premiers Paléologues. Etudes sur la polémique entre Théodore Métochites et Nicéphore Choumnos* (Brussels, 1962)

Spremić, M., 'Dva podatka Mari Branković' [Two facts about Mara Branković], *Istorijski Glasnik*, 1–2 (Belgrade, 1977), 71–80

Talbot, Alice-Mary Maffry, 'Blue-stocking nuns. Intellectual life in the convents of late Byzantium', in *Okeanos: Harvard Ukrainian Studies*, VII (*Essays Presented to Ihor Ševčenko*) (Cambridge, Mass., 1984), 604–18

Talbot, Alice-Mary Maffry, *Faith Healing in Late Byzantium. The posthumous miracles of the Patriarch Athanasios I of Constantinople by Theoktistos the Stoudite* (Brookline, Mass., 1983)

Talbot, Alice-Mary Maffry, 'Late Byzantine nuns: by choice or necessity?', *BF*, IX (1985), 59–102

Thalloczy, L. von, *Studien zur Geschichte Bosniens und Serbiens im Mittelalter* (Munich–Leipzig, 1914)

Théarvić, M., 'Notes de chronologie byzantines', *EO*, IX (1906), 298–300

Touratzoglou, J., 'Les sceaux byzantins en plomb de la collection Michael Ritzos au Musée de Thessaloniki', *Byzantina*, V (1973), 272–3

Treadgold, W., *The Byzantine Revival 780–842* (Stanford, Calif., 1988)

Treu, M. 'Manuel Holobolos', *BZ*, V (1906), 538–9

Trone, R., 'A Constantinopolitan double monastery of the fourteenth century: The Philanthropic Saviour', *Byzantine Studies/Etudes Byzantines*, X (1983), 81–7

Tsakopoulos, A., Περιγραφικὸς κατάλογος τῶν χειρογράφων τῆς βιβλιοθήκης τοῦ Οἰκουμενικοῦ Πατριαρχείου, II: 'Αγ. Τριάδος Χαλκῆς (Istanbul, 1956)

Turyn, A., *Codices Graeci Vaticani Saeculis XIII et XIV scripti annorumque notis instructi* (Vatican City, 1964)

Underwood, P., ed., *The Kariye Djami*, IV (Princeton, N.J., 1975)

Vakalopoulos, A. E., 'Die Frage der Glaubwürdigkeit der "Leichenrede auf L. Notaras" von Johannes Moschos (15. JH)', *BZ*, LII (1959), 13–21

Vakalopoulos, A. E., *History of Macedonia 1354–1833* (Thessaloniki, 1973)

Vakalopoulos, A. E., Ἱστορία τοῦ Νεοελληνισμοῦ, I, 2nd ed. (Thessaloniki, 1974)

Veludo (Veloudis), G., Ἑλλήνων Ὀρθοδόξων ἀποικία ἐν Βενετίᾳ, 2nd ed. (Venice, 1893)

Verpeaux, J., *Nicéphore Choumnos, homme d'état et humaniste byzantin (ca. 1250/1255–1327)* (Paris, 1959)

Verpeaux, J., 'Notes prosopographiques sur la famille Choumnos', *BS*, XX (1959), 252–66

Viani, Maria Christina Bandera, *Venezia. Museo delle Icone Bizantine e post Bizantine e Chiesa di San Giorgio dei Greci* (Bologna, 1988)

Vogel, M. and Gardthausen, V., *Die griechischen Schreiber des Mittelalters und der Renaissance* (Leipzig, 1909)

Vries-Van der Velden, Eva de, *L'Elite byzantine devant l'avance turque à l'époque de la guerre civile de 1341 à 1354* (Amsterdam, 1989)

Weiss, G., *Johannes Kantakuzenos – Aristokrat, Staatsmann, Kaiser und Mönch* (Wiesbaden, 1969)

Weyl, Anne Marie Carr, '*Women and Monasticism in Byzantium*. Introduction from an art historian', *BF*, IX (1985), 1–15

Wieruszowski, H., 'La Corte di Pietro d'Aragona', *ASI*, anno 96, vol. I (1938), 141–62

Wilson, N. G., 'Books and readers in Byzantium', *Byzantine Books and Bookmen* (Washington, D.C., 1975)

Wilson, N. G., *Scholars of Byzantium* (London, 1983)

Zacos, G. and Veglery, A., *Byzantine Lead Seals*, I (Basel, 1972)

INDEX